CHRÉTIEN DE TROYES

by

URBAN T. HOLMES

This book is not a compilation of all that has been written on Chrétien de Troyes. It is a presentation of what is actually known about him and the principal theories that are most widely accepted. Although the subject matter of Arthurian Romance has aroused much sharp discussion among scholars, Professor Holmes tries to harmonize opposing views when this can be done. Each chapter begins with statements made by Chrétien himself which are then followed by the views of leading scholars. Often the chapter closes with more individual interpretations proposed by the author himself.

Professor Holmes has been concerned with social history of the Middle Ages and this enables him to have a slightly differing view from others who have been working only in literary history. The bibliography given is widely eclectic which will enable the director of a course in which this book is used to influence his students in the direction that he prefers.

TWAYNE'S WORLD AUTHORS SERIES

A Survey of the World's Literature

Sylvia E. Bowman, Indiana University
GENERAL EDITOR

FRANCE

Maxwell A. Smith, Guerry Professor of French, Emeritus
The University of Chattanooga
Visiting Professor in Modern Languages
The Florida State University
EDITOR

Chrétien de Troyes

(TWAS 94)

TWAYNE'S WORLD AUTHORS SERIES (TWAS)

The purpose of TWAS is to survey the major writers —novelists, dramatists, historians, poets, philosophers, and critics—of the nations of the world. Among the national literatures covered are those of Australia, Canada, China, Eastern Europe, France, Germany, Greece, India, Italy, Japan, Latin America, New Zealand, Poland, Russia, Scandinavia, Spain, and the African nations, as well as Hebrew, Yiddish, and Latin Classical literatures. This survey is complemented by Twayne's United States Authors Series and English Authors Series.

The intent of each volume in these series is to present a critical-analytical study of the works of the writer; to include biographical and historical material that may be necessary for understanding, appreciation, and critical appraisal of the writer; and to present all material in clear, concise English—but not to vitiate the scholarly content of the work by doing so.

Chrétien de Troyes

By URBAN TIGNER HOLMES

University of North Carolina

Twayne Publishers, Inc.　::　New York

To the Memory of
EDWARD BILLINGS HAM
1902—1965

ABOUT THE AUTHOR

URBAN T. HOLMES is perhaps the senior active teacher of Mediaeval French literature and language in the United States. He began his studies with J. D. M. Ford, E. S. Sheldon, J. P. W. Crawford, C. H. Grandgent, Joseph Bédier, Mario Roques, Edmond Faral. His own students are now teaching Old French in many parts of America, including Canada. His first class in Old French was held at the University of Missouri in 1923. He moved to the University of North Carolina in 1925, where he was made a full professor in 1927 and a Kenan professor of Romance Philology in 1945. His books on Old French literature, and mediaeval French language and civilization, are used widely. He has always had a keen interest in mediaeval civilization in general, and this is manifest from the organizations in which he has been active. He is a Fellow of the Mediaeval Academy of America, the American Numismatic Society, the Society of Antiquaries (London), and the Royal Numismatic Society and a member of numerous other societies. He has received the Litt.D. from Washington and Lee and the University of Western Michigan, and is a chevalier of the Legion of Honor. In recent years he has been doing considerable lecturing on mediaeval topics from coast to coast.

Preface

This little volume is not a compilation of all that has been written on Chrétien de Troyes and his work. Such a compilation would be very useful as a book of reference; but it would not be effective as an introduction to the subject matter. For detailed examination of scholarly opinions the reader is advised to begin with James Douglas Bruce's *The Evolution of Arthurian Romance From the Beginnings Down to the Year 1300,* and with the *Bulletin bibliographique de la société internationale arthurienne.* Of great general value for bibliography are Jean Frappier's *Chrétien de Troyes: l'homme et l'oeuvre,* D. C. Cabeen's *A Critical Bibliography of French Literature,* Vol. I, and Robert Bossuat's *Manuel bibliographique de la littérature française du moyen âge,* with its supplements.

It may be remembered that the present writer has been working for many years as a social historian, with emphasis on medieval daily life, which is not the field of most who do research in Arthurian romance; this gives him a particular view of the world in which Chrétien lived.

There are many differences of opinion today about Arthurian material; but in the twelfth century also there were some who had different interpretations. Gerald the Welshman repeats a story that he heard at Caerleon. There was a clerk named Melerius who had long been disturbed in his mind:

> If the evil spirits oppressed him too much, the Gospel of St. John was placed on his bosom, when, like birds, they immediately vanished; but when that book was removed, and the History of the Britons, by Geoffrey [of Monmouth] was substituted in its place, they instantly reappeared in greater numbers, and remained a longer time than usual on his body and on that book. (*Itinerary through Wales*, trans. R. C. Hoare [London: Dent, 1908], p. 53)

This book has been written over a number of years, when the author could find leisure for it. Warm appreciation must be expressed for the assistance of Dr. William Kibler, a former student of the author's, who has done much of the mechanical work in formulating the notes, and who has served as critic, indicating details that should be emphasized. The opinions expressed, however, are those of the author, who takes all responsibility for them.

URBAN TIGNER HOLMES

University of North Carolina

Contents

Chronology

573   Owein son of Urian at Battle of Armterid.

600   First mention of Arthur (in Aneirin's *Gododdin*).

1093– St. Anselm is archbishop of Canterbury.
1109

1096– The First Crusade.
1099

1125– William of Malmesbury's histories of the kings of Britain,
1142   of the English bishops, and of Glastonbury Abbey.

1125– Thibaut II is count of Champagne.
1152

1126   Henry of Blois becomes abbot of Glastonbury. Count Thibaut of Champagne marries Mathilda of Carinthia.

1128   The Knights Templars receive their organization at Troyes.

1129   Henry of Blois becomes bishop of Winchester, while remaining abbot of Glastonbury.

1129– Geoffrey of Monmouth teaching at Oxford.
1152

1136   Geoffrey of Monmouth's *History of the Kings of Britain*.

1137   Louis VII becomes French king.

1139   Gaimar's *History of the English*.

1147– The Second Crusade.
1148

1147   Henry of Champagne knighted at Constantinople.

1147– Peter Comestor teaches in Cathedral school at Troyes.
1164

1148   Rabbinical schools move from Ramerupt to Troyes.

1149   Henry Plantagenet knighted at Carlisle by Scottish king.

1152– Henry I (the Liberal) is count of Champagne.
1181

1152	Eleanor of Aquitaine marries Henry Plantagenet.
1153	St. Bernard dies. The end of Stephen-Mathilda War in England.
1154	Henry of Blois goes in exile to Cluny Abbey.
1154– 1189	Henry Plantagenet becomes Henry II of England.
1156– 1159	Hadrian IV, an Englishman, is pope.
1155	Wace finishes his *Brut*.
1159	Marie, daughter of Eleanor of Aquitaine, marries Henry I of Champagne.
1164	Thomas Becket exiled from England.
1170	Murder of Thomas Becket at Canterbury (December 29). Invasion of Ireland by the Anglo-Welsh.
1171	Henry of Blois, bishop and abbot, dies.
1173– 1174	Sons of Henry II of England rebel. Eleanor confined in Old Sarum.
1179	Louis VII shows special favor towards the Jews.
1180	Louis VII dies. Manuel of Constantinople dies.
1180– 1223	Philip Augustus is king of France, and is severe with the Jews.
1181	Philip of Flanders becomes more powerful; enters into coalition against Philip Augustus.
1187	Saladin takes Jerusalem after Battle of Hittin.
1189– 1192	Third Crusade.
1191	Supposed tomb of Arthur and Guenevere opened at Glastonbury.
1198	Marie de Champagne dies.
1204	Eleanor of Aquitaine dies at Fontevrault.

CHAPTER 1

Chretien de Troyes

A great deal has been written about Chrétien in the past hundred years. Because there is so little positive information about him and the circumstances surrounding his work, there has been much argument among scholars. It is our task to harmonize as much of this as we can. Where this is not possible we will try to present all sides of the case, and we hope that readers will be tolerant. At the same time, we must try to maintain a freshness of approach; so these pages will present a certain amount of material that is new.

I Identity of the Poet

The first problem is the identity of the poet. We will begin with statements made by Chrétien in his works and then proceed to opinions held by various scholars. The poet names himself "Crestien," and little more, in all his romances save the oldest one, the *Erec and Enide*, in which he calls himself "Crestien de Troyes":

"Therefore," says Crestien de Troyes, "it is right that one should give thought and try to speak and do well. He [Crestien] makes from

a simple tale of adventure a fine combination of plot and meaning.
. . . Now I shall begin a story which will last as long as Christianity;
Crestien boasts that he will do this." (vss. 23–26) [1]

Another poet, Gerbert de Montreuil, used this more complete
designation in his continuation of Chrétien's *Perceval:* "Crestien
de Troyes, who began the story of Perceval, told us this; but
Death overtook him and did not let him bring it to an end"
(vss. 6984–87). [2]

It is agreed by many scholars, including Gaston Paris and
Reto R. Bezzola, that the surname "de Troyes" was more apt
to have been used when Chrétien was not actually resident in
the Troyes area. It can be assumed that when he was surrounded
by people who knew him well, the name "Crestien" was sufficient.
Some readers may recall that in a later medieval period François
Villon had two additional descriptive names, François de Mont-
corbier and François des Loges, which we are unable to explain
today. Undoubtedly, while he was with his friends in Paris
he was known simply as François. As we shall postulate further
in Chapter IV, Chrétien was probably not in France when he
wrote the *Erec and Enide.*

II *Probable Order of His Writings*

In his second major work, the *Cligés,* Chrétien lists his earlier
compositions:

He wrote about Erec and Enide, and composed the Commands
of Ovid and his Art of Love in the vulgar tongue, and who wrote
also the "Shoulder Bite"—and about Mark and blond Yseut, and about
the transformation of the hoopoe, the swallow, and the nightingale,
he now begins once more a new tale . . . This narrative which I
wish to retell I found written in a book on the shelves of My Lord
Saint Peter at Beauvais. The plot was taken from there, out of which
Crestiens has made this romance. . . . (vss. 1–8, 18–22)

We cannot be sure of the relative order of these early produc-
tions; but we know from this passage that he began his poetic
career with:

1. Ovid's *Art of Love*
2. Probably Ovid's *Remedy of Love*
3. The story of Pelops and his father Tantalus ("Shoulder Bite")
4. Either the whole or a part of the Tristan story (Mark and Yseut)
5. Ovid's *Philomela* tale (hoopoe, swallow, and nightingale)
6. *Erec and Enide*
7. *Cligés*

In the second quarter of the twelfth century, as suggested in these early works, it was becoming fashionable to adapt stories from Latin into Romance. Chrétien's contemporary, Marie de France, had thought of doing the same, "but it would hardly have been worthwhile; so many others were doing this" (Prologue, vss. 28–32).[3]

It is extremely likely that the *Cligés* was followed by the *Lancelot* or *Knight of the Cart*, which Chrétien wrote for Marie, the daughter of Eleanor of Aquitaine, after her marriage to Count Henry II of Champagne in 1159. He says in this connection:

Because my lady of Champagne wants me to undertake a romance I will do this very willingly . . . Crestien begins this book, for which the Countess transmits to him the plot and the allegory; he sees to it that he adds nothing more except his effort and his intention. (vss. 1–3, 24–29)

Chrétien did not finish this particular romance. Another poet added at the close of it:

Godefroi de Leigny, clerk, has ended this tale of the Cart, but let no one blame him for adding on to Crestien; he has done this with the consent of Crestien who began it. [Godefroi] has added that part of the narrative which begins where Lancelot was imprisoned behind the wall. (vss. 7102–9).

Next, we place the *Yvain* or *Knight of the Lion.* There is no proof positive that this was the work of Chrétien; but nobody has ever been disposed to doubt it:

Crestien ends in this way his romance of the Knight with the Lion. He has never heard any more about this, nor will you hear anything further [dear reader] unless some one wants to add what is false. (vss. 6817–22)

It is strange that the *Guillaume d'Angleterre* is not accepted as the work of Chrétien de Troyes by all critics.[4] It has an ascription which is quite similar in expression to that found in the *Yvain*:

Crestien wishes to begin without adding or removing anything . . . Someone who wishes to look for English tales would find at Bury-Saint-Edmund's one that is quite trustworthy, which is charming and true. To prove this he should go there to find it, if he desires. Crestien is speaking—and he is used to speaking . . . (vss. 1–2, 11–18)

It is quite evident from this statement that the Chrétien who composed the *Guillaume d'Angleterre* was a poet of considerable reputation. It is extremely unlikely that this Chrétien was another distinguished writer of romance and not our Chrétien de Troyes.

The most important, and most controversial, romance attributed to Chrétien de Troyes is the *Conte dou Graal* or *Perceval*. Here again the poet himself does not pinpoint his identity; but it is confirmed by others. He says:

Crestien sows and scatters the seed of a romance which he now begins. . . . and he sows it in so favorable a place that this must be to great advantage. He does this for the finest gentleman who is subject to Rome: this is Count Philip of Flanders . . . (vss. 1–2, 7–13)

One cannot be absolutely sure of the order in which these works of Chrétien's were composed, but the order in which we have presented them is not unlikely: *Erec and Enide, Cligés, Lancelot, Yvain, Guillaume d'Angleterre,* and the *Conte del Graal*. In addition to these larger works, two lyric poems preserved in *chansonniers* U and C are held to be his;[5] for in the margins of U a later hand has added an attribution to Chrétien de Troyes. Granted this is correct, Chrétien is the oldest lyric poet of northern France whose name is known to us. The range of dating for him lies within the period 1160–90, with the majority of scholars today placing his chief activity in the 1170's. There remains another speculation with respect to his work. We know from the passage in the *Cligés* cited above that he wrote a *Tristan* and certain Ovidian adaptations. These are presumably lost; but there is good possibility that one of his Ovidian works is perserved. This, a *Philomena* in Champenois dialect, was incorporated into a vast Ovidian compilation dating around 1307.[6] Gaston Paris was the first to call attention to it, in *Romania*, XIII (1884), 399 ff. The most interesting factor here is that the poem is signed by a "Crestiens li Gois." More will be said about this in Chapter III.

Information on Chrétien de Troyes's life and career, and on these works that we have listed, must be speculation. It is remarkable that we find as much uniformity of opinion as we do.

III   *Ideas of Gaston Paris*

Gaston Paris assumed that Chrétien was born in Troyes (Aube).[7] He accepted the surviving *Philomena* as Chrétien's own work, and explained the "li Gois" as a name of unclear origin which Chrétien could have used as a youth in his native town. "*Il fit des études cléricales*," wrote Paris, which obviously means that Paris thought Chrétien belonged to the clerical class. Paris also thought that the *Commandement Ovide* mentioned in the *Cligés* list meant the *Remedia Amoris* of Ovid; he was not sure whether the "Shoulder Bite" tale was the Pelops and Tantalus story. As we have just stated, Paris believed that the *Erec and Enide* was not written at Troyes, because of the adding of "de Troyes" to Chrétien's name. A very original suggestion from Gaston Paris was that Chrétien could have been a herald. He cites this passage from the *Cligés*: "And know that then there was said for the first time, Now he is come who will measure [*Or est venuz qui aunera*]. Our teacher was the herald who taught us to say this; he himself was the first to say it" (vss. 5591–94). (A herald seldom had a full-time job. Some heralds were minstrels and others were minor clerks in simple tonsure attached to a court.)

Gaston Paris did not believe that Chrétien wrote a full romance on the Tristan theme; he suggests that he composed only a short episodic poem on King Mark and Queen Iseut. The name Tristan is not mentioned in the *Cligés* list, and elsewhere Chrétien speaks slightingly of the loves of Tristan and Iseut (notably in the *Cligés*). Besides, no other poet of Chrétien's time has ever referred to such a work by Chrétien, whose superiority in this subject matter would surely have drawn attention.

Gaston Paris was convinced that Chrétien had visited England. The grouping of Southampton and Winchester, and the mentions of Shoreham, Wallingford, Oxford, and Windsor on the Thames prove this. The listing of these English towns in the *Cligés* is done according to proper pattern and does not suggest a random listing which a purely Continental poet might have had at hand. Paris believed that the *Cligés* was composed in 1170 and the *Erec* in about 1168. The *Lancelot* he assigned to 1172 and the *Yvain* the same time (before 1173), since Nûr-ed-Din of Aleppo, who is mentioned as living, died on May 15, 1173. Paris did not want to believe that the *Lancelot* came very soon after 1164, which he accepted as the date of the marriage of Marie to Henry I of Champagne. He thought that an "adulterous theme" could not have been proposed by a recent bride. He believed the *Perceval* preceded 1180 since Philip of Flanders was appointed a regent of France at that date and this rank is not mentioned in the praise of Philip which comes early in the *Perceval*. *Paris* felt also that Chrétien would have spoken of Philip's journey to the Holy Land in 1177–78. He dated the *Perceval* preferably in 1174–75. This means that, for Gaston Paris, Chrétien died in 1175, before he could complete the Grail story. Since Paris assigned the *Philomena* to 1160, this gave Chrétien a writing career of not more than fifteen years.

According to Gaston Paris, Chrétien knew the *Roman de Thébes*, the *Eneas*, the *Roman de Troie*, the *Apollonius of Tyre*, the *Metamorphoses* of Ovid, and, of course, Ovid's *Art of Love*. But it was the Tristan story that first attracted Chrétien to Celtic material. He probably used the *Tristan* of La Chévre.[8] The love of Lancelot and Guenevere was inspired by that of Tristan and Iseut. Paris considered that the *Lancelot*, which contained some Celtic mythology, was ill-composed. The *Cligés*, he believed, was founded upon an Oriental tale. It should be noted that Gaston Paris did not support the attribution of the *Guillaume d'Angleterre* to Chrétien.

IV   *Wendelin Foerster*

We must also consider Wendelin Foerster's mature opinion on these matters.[9] Foerster opposed Paris' belief that the young bride Marie de Champagne could not have encouraged an "adulterous" courtly love theme for Chrétien. He accepted the *Guillaume d'Angleterre* as Chrétien's work, dating it shortly after the *Cligés*; in this he agreed with Maurice Wilmotte.[10] The relative order that Foerster assigned to the romances was: Ovidian adaptations, *Tristan, Erec, Cligés, Guillaume d'Angleterre, Lancelot, Yvain,* and *Perceval.* He insisted strongly that the *Cligés* was "anti-Tristan," Chrétien's antithesis to the adulterous Tristan narrative he had so recently completed. Foerster found parallels between the *Cligés* and the anonymous romance *Athis and Prophilias.* He could see no particular thesis in the *Guillaume d'Angleterre.* On the other hand, he admitted religious inspiration in the *Perceval,* stating that this was presented obscurely. Foerster contended that all of Chrétien's poems were composed from shortly before 1160 until not much after 1170: the *Erec* probably came soon after Wace's *Brut* (1155), and was influenced by the *Thébes, Troie,* and *Eneas* romances (which Foerster assigned to 1150–60); the *Lancelot* and the *Yvain* could not have been earlier than 1164 (the date proposed by D'Arbois de Jubainville for Marie's marriage) or later than 1173-74 (the date of Nûr-ed-din's death); conceivably the *Perceval* could have been composed any time between 1168 and 1191, but Foerster preferred 1171. Most important of all— Foerster admitted very little Celtic material in any of these romances; for him they were "continental tales."

On Chrétien's career Foerster had these remarks to make. Chrétien was clerically trained, although it cannot be proved that he was a cleric. (Foerster was not precise on the definition of a clerk. One who had attended the schools was certainly a clerk.) Foerster did not agree that Chrétien had necessarily been in England. He thought that English merchants could have carried to France the small amount of knowledge about England which Chrétien displayed.

V Stefan Hofer

Next we consider the beliefs of Stefan Hofer.[11] He suggests that Chrétien was a court poet who entered the service of Marie de Champagne in 1165. (Again this is a date suggested by 1164 as the marriage date for Marie and Henry of Champagne.) There he began to write the *Erec;* then he continued with the Ovidian adaptations. Afterwards he produced the *Cligés* (around 1172), the *Lancelot,* the *Yvain,* and the *Guillaume d'Angleterre,* in this order. In 1181–82 he left Marie's service, following the death of her husband, and entered the service of Philip of Flanders—for whom he wrote the *Perceval.* Hofer does not insist that the *Guillaume d'Angleterre* was written by another poet named Chrétien. He too agrees that there could have been only one outstanding writer of romance at this time who signed himself "Crestien." He does not allow that Chrétien was a canon of Saint-Loup, the Augustinian monastery in Troyes (a possibility that was first proposed by L. A. Vigneras).[12] It seems to Hofer that Chrétien was not genuinely inspired by clerical ideas.

VI Jean Frappier

The best opinion of that group of Arthurian scholars designated as *Celtisants* (because they assume a dominating Celtic influence for Arthurian material) is given by Jean Frappier—first in his *Chrétien de Troyes: l'homme et l'oeuvre (loc. cit.),*[13] and more recently in Chapter XV of Roger Sherman Loomis' *Arthurian Literature in the Middle Ages.*[14] Frappier does not believe that Chrétien was the originator of Arthurian romance, nor does he concede that he was necessarily a native of Troyes—he may have lived in that city only for a short time. Frappier disagrees with the suggestion that Chrétien was a herald, but accepts that he was clerically trained (which must mean, of course, that he was a clerk). However, Frappier is not inclined to believe that Chrétien was a priest, and does not consider it certain that Chrétien visited England. Frappier accepts the surviving *Philomena* as Chrétien's work; but he does not accept the *Guillaume d'Angleterre*. He does not emphasize the significance of the "adulterous passion" in the *Lancelot*, although he admits that Chrétien was obsessed by a reaction against the dishonorable love of the *Tristan* in all his works before the *Perceval*. All of them were anti-Tristan. On the whole, Frappier denies that Chrétien was much concerned with symbolism, arguing that the poet was more interested in lucidity and psychological reactions. He insists that the name Crestien was very common. He is convinced that Chrétien had heared many Celtic tales and poems retold by minstrels from Celtic territories. (He does not specify Brittany only, as some have done.) He states that Chrétien retold this material with great skill—intermingling the fantastic with the real.

In giving dates, Frappier follows Hofer and Fourrier.[15] The *Erec* he places in 1170, the *Cligés* about 1176. He concludes that the *Lancelot* and the *Yvain* were done concurrently in 1177-81, and the *Perceval* after 1181. Frappier is not convinced that Chrétien left the service of Marie to serve Philip of Flanders. After all, Philip was courting Marie at Troyes in 1182.

VII General Agreement

When these statements of some of the leading Arthurian scholars are compared, it becomes evident that they are in accord on many points. They agree that Chrétien had clerical training (which must mean that he was in lower orders, at least), that he was born or lived for a long while in Troyes (Aube), that he was attached for most of his career to the court at Troyes, and that he composed there his *Lancelot, Cligés,* and *Yvain,* and possibly the *Guillaume d'Angleterre*. Their estimates of the years of his employment vary, beginning as early as 1160 and ending as late as 1182. The critics are divided as to whether Chrétien visited England at some time during his early career; but all agree that this is not improbable. They are not in strict accord as to whether the *Erec and Enide* was composed away from the Troyes area, whether the *Perceval* was written for Philip of Flanders away from Troyes, whether the extant *Philomena* poem is Chrétien's poem, and in estimating the amount of Celtic and Classical influence.

VIII *Present Author's Views*

Our own approach differs somewhat from those of these predecessors.[16] We emphasize the need for examining carefully the
medieval background, including the social customs, the physical
environment, the personal associations, and the psychology (as
far as it can be ascertained, for it differs from the modern in
many aspects). Much that can be established in this way is subjective. Little of this can be convincing to someone who thinks
along a different pattern; but efforts of this kind are worth a try.

One of the important facts about the city of Troyes in the
twelfth century is that it was a center for Jewish commerce
and teaching. The school of talmudic learning established in
the town of Ramerupt by the great Rashi, and others, was continued in Troyes by his sons-in-law. Troyes consisted of two
divisions: the old citadel with its Roman walls, and the *portus*
or merchant city which lay beside it, first fortified by earth and
wooden palisade, and later by stone ramparts. Within the citadel
was the count's donjon, the great Augustinian Abbey of Saint-
Loup, the cathedral church of Saint-Pierre, the Jewish quarter
surrounding the synagogue, the count's palace with its chapel
of Saint-Estienne attached, and a certain number of ordinary
dwelling houses and businesses. The *portus*, on the other hand,
had a wide spread of streets, many religious houses, two market
places, another synagogue, the site of the great fair, and the
donjon of the viscount. The Jewish talmudic school was established in the quarter inside the citadel. Between the cathedral
and the Abbey of Saint-Loup, along the stretch of the town
wall, was the cathedral school. It is probable that, as a clerk
in lower orders or simple tonsure, Chrétien attended classes in
this school—perhaps while Peter Comestor was the master.[17]

IX *Chrétien's Name*

An interesting problem is presented by the name "Chrétien,"
or rather "Cristianus." Many documents of the second half of
the twelfth century are preserved in the archives at Troyes and
at Chaumont. These have been carefully examined by Professor

John Benton, now at California Institute of Technology.[18] Also, there are typical large lists of names such as the roster of men left to garrison Dublin Castle in 1184 by Henry II of England. Examination of all such material reveals that "Christianus," or "Crestien," as a baptismal name was extremely uncommon at this time. There are a few examples where "Crestien" as an added surname, or descriptive name, does occur. Thomas Becket, when he fled from England in 1164, after the dispute at Clarendon, assumed the descriptive name "Crestien." There is a case on record where a Jewish physician when baptized was given the baptismal name "Crestien." Professor John Mahoney has argued that because of this last *proved* example it can never be reasonably denied that a Jew baptized as an adult would have taken this particular name.[19]

Several conclusions may be drawn from this. Chrétien could have received his name as a baptized Jew—particularly in view of the general environment which existed in Troyes. Also, in view of the relatively small number of inhabitants of Troyes who would have been engaged in the writing of romances, and because of the scarcity of the name, it can hardly be claimed that there were numerous romance poets in that region with the name Crestien.

In 1172 there was a clerk named Chrétien who was granted a benefice at Saint-Maclou in Bar-sur-Aube (twenty-five miles from Troyes) by Count Henry and his wife Marie. It is logically possible to assume that this clerk was our writer of romances, thus rewarded by his patrons. This benefice meant that the incumbent was in priest's orders.

It is of little value to quibble whether Chrétien was in the service of Count Henry, or only of his wife Marie de Champagne—or whether a man who had written slightly immoral romances was worthy of being a chaplain. Henry and Marie both presided at the court in Troyes, and romantic tales have been narrated by priests in all ages. It is *reasonable* to suggest that Chrétien de Troyes was Chrétien de Saint-Maclou at Bar-sur-Aube. This collegiate church had been founded by Count Henry and his wife. (The church is still standing, although its arches are now supported by emergency braces. It is no longer used. The interior is twelfth-century and it takes no great imagination to dream that our Chrétien de Troyes once sat in its choir.)

X   *Chrétien in England*

It has been mentioned above that most scholars believe Chré-tien paid a visit to England, early in his career. A special link between Troyes and England was Henry of Blois, abbot of Glas-tonbury (1126–71) and bishop of Winchester (1129–71). This prelate was a brother of Thibaut II of Champagne and therefore the uncle of Count Henry the Liberal, to whom we will be constantly referring in these pages. He was also a brother of King Stephen of England. He began as a monk at Cluny.

Almost everyone admits that the Abbey of Glastonbury had an important role in the launching of Arthurian legends. Perhaps there was a monk named Caradoc who lived there and had some responsibility for this. It was he who wrote the *Vita Gildae* which, as we shall see in our Chapter VI, is credited with being the source for the Guenevere Abduction story. We suggest that after the young Chrétien had won his first laurels in Troyes, by his adaptations of Ovid, it was arranged that he should go to England in the train of Bishop Henry of Blois. This would have brought him into immediate contact with Glastonbury, and he would not have been long in gleaning some of the early details of an Arthurian setting. It is generally accepted that the Tristan legend made its way down from Scotland into that area and into Cornwall.[20] It is probable that Chrétien was aware of Scotland; he certainly used Scottish place names in the *Guillaume d'Angleterre*.

Both Geoffrey of Monmouth and William of Malmesbury had many contacts with Henry of Blois—and in turn Bishop Henry had his roots in the Champagne area. In his *History of the Kings of Britain*[21] (composed *ca.* 1136), Geoffrey places the first battle of Arthur against the king of the Romans on the Aube River, and the second battle near Langres (which means in the vicinity of Bar-sur-Aube).

We suggest that when Chrétien returned from England to the court at Troyes, where interest in Chrétien's *Erec and Enide*, and also in Byzantine legends, was running high, he composed the *Cligés*, followed by his *Lancelot* and *Yvain* early in the 1170's. This was soon followed by another Byzantine theme in the *Guillaume d'Angleterre*. At this point Chrétien may have been glad to assume ecclesiastical duties—at Saint-Maclou (?)—from which he was aroused a decade later by the young, powerful Philip of Flanders, to write the *Conte dou Graal*. Philip was courting the widowed Marie de Champagne at the time. Death overtook Chrétien in the 1180's while he was still at work on this very long poem.

XI *Chrétien's Method*

In medieval scholarship today there is a desire to look deeply into an author's work to formulate what we can about the man himself and his psychological reactions. This is difficult to do and one can never be sure of the conclusions that are drawn. Thus, D. W. Robertson has proposed that Chrétien, like Ovid, was an ironist in his treatment of love—notably in the *Cligés*. Mrs. Barbara Sargent, in a very recent study, expresses belief that Chrétien's principal characters are always double—what they are or have been versus what they want to be. When they are changed they may assume another name: the Knight of the Cart becomes Lancelot; Yvain becomes the Knight of the Lion; Fenice the wife of the Greek emperor becomes the Love of Cligés; Erec becomes a new Erec after his trials in the company of Enide. Mrs. Sargent thinks that Perceval is, in a way, redoubled by Gawain; but, alas, we do not have the end of the *Conte dou Graal*. In this way each principal character has his or her second person.[22]

Various scholars have described Chrétien's style, which is equivalent to saying "the way he thought." Perhaps one of the most sensitive of these critics is Julian Harris of the University of Wisconsin. We now summarize briefly some of his remarks:[23]

The medieval conception of perspective and composition was quite different from ours. Chrétien's individual characters are often introduced for a while without being named. Many minor characters, and minor episodes—which have little bearing on the web of the story—are minutely described and made to seem important. There are unexpected changes of pace in this way—and, in turn, what should be major episodes seem to be passed over quickly. Chrétien has a vigorous style, interspersed with many personal asides. He is extremely fond of similes, "parallelisms," for example, when Yvain kills the giant the spectators rush out to examine the giant "as dogs run to a fallen animal" (p. 41). In telling his stories, Chrétien passes very easily from narrative to dialogue; to affirmation, to negation, to doubt, and to making use of inverted sentences. He often interjects paradoxical statements, which he then proceeds to prove by dialectic. He has keen dramatic sense. This is well shown in that scene of the *Yvain* where the girl who brings relief to the naked and mad hero pretends that she has just chanced to pass by—in order to save him embarrassment! Chrétien often prefers to describe an observer's reaction to a scene, rather than give a straight description (for example, Laudine's charm is pictured through Yvain's eyes). Chrétien is always gay, natural, and good-humored. Like most poets of his day he did not hesitate to introduce oddities and the supernatural where, within the composition of his poem, this impossibility could appear probable. He mingles the tragic and the comic.

An approach to Chrétien's content which is too difficult for the average reader is in Erich Köhler's "Ideal und Wirklichkeit in der höfischen Epik," in the *Archiv für das Studium der neueren Sprachen*, CXCVII (1960), 236–40. Köhler seeks to explain this courtly epic production in the light of its historico-sociological and cultural-historical manifestations.[24]

CHAPTER 2

The Twelfth Century and the Origins of the Romance

T HREE dominating spheres of influence made possible the rise of the romance form—and incidentally of Chrétien de Troyes and his Arthurian themes. These were the great spread of territory under the Anglo-Norman king of England; the "look" towards Germany, Byzantium, and Sicily which had developed in eastern France (including Champagne); and the immense rise of the schools and other clerical activity in the cathedral centers; this last was the climax of what is called the Twelfth-Century Renaissance.

At the very heart of the English kingdom were the Celtic speaking peoples: the Welsh, the Cornish, and the inhabitants of the former kingdom of Strathclyde—extending down the west coast of England, southward from Carlisle—to which we must add, in 1158, the Bretons of continental Brittany. The Celts had no political power—the Welsh, in particular, were often in revolt—but their very presence and the distinctiveness of their language and customs made them an important factor among the Anglo-Normans and the people of Saxon descent. Welsh oral material began to be written down about 1090, and there was contact with Ireland (notably Wexford and Waterford) through Bristol and the Welsh ports.

Champagne and lower Lorraine looked much towards the Rhineland and this meant associations with the German emperor,

Byzantium, and Palermo. This was not a relationship with which the average person was much concerned, but it affected the ruling class, the minstrels, and some of the men of letters. Interestingly enough, the people of Flanders felt closer to the Holy Land and to the whole Crusade movement, probably because of their pride in Godefroy of Bouillon. The Crusade epics started there.

On the new rise of the cathedral and monastic schools, and on all that this entailed, many have written convincingly.[1] From the close of the eleventh century, beginning with St. Anselm of Canterbury and St. Anselm of Laon, there was a vigorous awakening of theology, law, letters, and science. This was particularly strong among the Anglo-Normans (in England and on the Continent), but it flourished also at Paris, Chartres, Orleans, and many other centers. Not only did many people acquire a pleasurable interest in ancient mythology and literary themes; the whole climate of literary taste began to change. After the middle of the century there was a reaction against incessant adaptation of ancient Classical material. This, we believe, is where Marie de France and Chrétien began. They purposely introduced into the French vernacular a different subject matter, which we call the *matière de Bretagne*, as opposed to the *matière de Rome*. Fortunately, those who had developed the *matière de Rome* had begun by adopting newer forms of narrative: the romance and the *conte*. These were at hand for Chrétien and Marie de France.

We remind our readers of another factor. This was the prevalence in eastern France and in the Rhineland of Jewish schools and wealth. The present writer believes that this too had considerable influence on some writers, but the idea has been so vigorously opposed by many of our colleagues that we leave it as an open question.

I *Byzantine Influence*

We begin a more detailed sketch of the twelfth century with Byzantium and with Manuel Comnenos, who was the Byzantine emperor from 1143 to 1180.[2] His mother was Hungarian and he himself married a German princess, Bertha of Sulzbach, in 1146. He was famed for rash and bold knighthood, although he did not show particular military genius as a leader. The Greek emperor's reputation for chivalry was so great that St. Bernard advised young Henry of Champagne to be knighted by him while on the Crusade (1147), presumably at the Blanchernae Palace at at the entrance to the Golden Horn. Besides fighting, Manuel's favorite pursuits were magic and astrology. In 1147 his forces were attacked by those of Roger II of Sicily. The Normans from Sicily took Corfu for a brief time and plundered Thebes in Greece proper, which was the center for the silk industry. A number of Greek silk workers were carried off to Palermo; but Manuel finally repulsed these attacks, with the aid of the Venetians.

When Roger II of Sicily died in 1154 he was succeeded by William I. Manuel felt that the time was propitious to retaliate against the Normans. Frederick Barbarossa was now emperor of Germany, and was also in contention for the crown of Sicily. After Frederick returned to Germany following his coronation, Manuel and Pope Hadrian struck together in southern Italy. Unexpectedly, the apparently weak William I of Sicily responded quickly, destroying the Byzantines at Brindisi in May, 1156. The Pope then changed sides and made peace with the Sicilians, supporting them against Frederick Barbarossa. Peace was concluded with Byzantium in 1158—but the Byzantine Manuel, betrayed by the Pope, remained a close ally of the German Frederick Barbarossa.

II *English Domination*

Western influence continued strong at the Byzantine court, while at Rome English influence was dominant. Pope Hadrian was an Englishman, Nicholas Brakespear, but English interests had already been strong in Rome for at least ten years prior to his election in 1154. Pope Eugenius III, a Cistercian and an intimate of St. Bernard, kept many Englishmen about him. Robert Pullen was his chancellor (1144–46), and Nicholas Brakespear had been an influential cardinal since 1149. John of Salisbury was the papal clerk from 1146 until 1154, when he passed over to the service of Archbishop Theobald of Canterbury. There was a brilliant group at Canterbury, known as the *Cantuarienses.* Archbishop Theobald was greatly concerned with law—canon law—and this interest was shared by his entourage, which included Thomas Becket, archdeacon of Canterbury since 1154. Archbishop Theobald, Thomas Becket, and John of Salisbury provoked a brilliant intellectual life in England.

The Second Crusade (1147–48) was a rank failure, militarily speaking, but it initiated many lines of transmission between Byzantium and the extreme West, through Sicily, Rome, and Germany. Manuel Comnenos caused his son, Alexius II, to marry a princess from France, Agnes, the sister of King Philip Augustus—but this was later in the century.

Henry Plantagenet became duke of Normandy in 1149, and was knighted that year at Carlisle by his grand-uncle, King Malcolm of Scotland. Henry had received an unusually good education in letters, science, and dialectic from Peter of Saintes, Adelard of Bath, and William of Conches. King Louis VII of France resented the activity in Normandy of this young rival; there followed French-English hostilities in 1149–51, in which Eustache of Boulogne, the son of King Stephen of England, took sides with the French. On September 3, 1151, Geoffrey Plantagenet died and Henry, his son, became duke of Anjou as well as of Normandy. On March 31, 1152, the marriage of Louis VII to Eleanor of Aquitaine was annulled by a council at Beaugency. Henry Plantagenet lost no time; although Eleanor was eleven years older than he was, he married the heiress of Aquitaine in May, 1152. In 1153 Henry was accepted as heir to the throne of England. When King Stephen died in September, 1154, Henry was crowned as Henry II of England. During the next twenty-five years, which saw the growth of the romance form, Henry II of England and Louis VII of France were constant adversaries.

III *Difficulties in France*

Louis VII was a pious, monklike king who was hardly able to cope with his vigorous rival, Henry II. In 1152–54, when public opinion was on Louis' side (Henry had married Eleanor without the consent of his nominal overlord, Louis VII), he tried to check him. This attempt was pitiful, and soon Henry II of

England owned all of western France from the Somme to the Pyrenees, excepting Brittany. He got Brittany in 1158. By 1159 he controlled Toulouse, which means the southeastern part of France. In 1159 Ramon-Balaguer IV of Barcelona made advances to Henry. When Thierry d'Alsace, count of Flanders, went to the Holy Land in 1157, he left the care of his lands not in the hands of his feudal lord, Louis—but with the English king. Traitors soon developed: Thibaut of Blois (brother of Henry I of Champagne) passed over to the English in 1159; so did Simon of Evreux. Louis could hardly ride safely out of Paris. Thus in this decade of the 1150's we find what we might call the "Pax Anglicana" enveloping almost all of France proper.

Louis VII saved himself by his marriages—and by becoming the protector of Thomas Becket who, as archbishop of Canterbury in 1162, soon made himself a thorn in the side of England. In 1154 Louis countered the marriage of Henry to Eleanor by marrying Constance, the daughter of Alfonso VII of Castile. He had two daughters by her, Marie and Alix. She died in 1160, and he promptly took another wife, Adèle of Champagne, the youngest child of Thibaut II of Champagne. This last marriage brought to Louis' side her four brothers: Henry I of Champagne, Thibaut of Blois, Estienne of Sancerre, and Bishop Guillaume of Sens. In September, 1158, Henry II, and his chancellor, Thomas Becket, came to Paris in great triumph to carry to their own domain Louis' eldest daughter, Marie, who was betrothed to the young Prince Henry (b. 1155). This was probably the highest point of English fortunes in France. Marie's dowry was now claimed—the French Vexin adjacent to Normandy. In the early 1160's Henry also took Alix, to become the bride of prince Richard (b. 1157); but King Henry's flagrant misbehavior with this girl, as well as his treatment of Archbishop Thomas Becket, was now putting the English in a bad light.

We have tried to sketch this history of the 1150's in as palatable a form as possible. Before we finish, something must be said of the activity of Frederick Barbarossa of Germany. He had become Emperor in 1151. In 1156 he married Beatrice of Burgundy, right on the doorstep of France; thus Odo II, her father, became his ally. The counts of Mâcon and Châlon, the lord of Beaujeu, and the archbishop of Lyon Frederick, all changed their allegiance to Frederick; and Henry I of Champagne, Chrétien's patron, made secret alliance with him. All this changed slightly in 1160 with Louis VII of France's marriage to Adèle of Champagne.

IV Norman Learning

To sum up, the territory of the king of France was being encroached upon from every side by the English and the Germans. Englishmen (which means especially the Anglo-Normans) were currently influential in Rome. We have already spoken of English interest in the literature of ancient Rome, and, from their territories in continental France, there came steady pressure in this direction. One may well ask why so much learning was encouraged by them—and especially in the vernacular language. Undoubtedly the Anglo-Normans were a very enterprising people. They were the Yankees of the eleventh and twelfth centuries, perhaps because they were a mixed people. Also, there is the factor that they were *parvenus*. The descendants of those who had fought with William the Conqueror felt the need of "boasting" about their ancestors and their deeds, and of spreading abroad as much learning as they could.

Cornelis de Boer has epitomized this:

In the west of France in the mid-twelfth century there was a true school of imitators of Classical Antiquity, which left us three important works of which the last, the *Roman de Troie*, is dated 1165 . . . The lost *lai* of Orpheus predates Marie de France, who speaks of it in her [sic] *Lai de l'Espine*; the *Roman de Troie* brings to our attention the existence of a poem on *Hero and Leander*; a tale about *Tantalus* is mentioned in *Guillaume d'Angleterre*. We know that the story of *Piramus and Thisbé* was very widespread by the second half of the twelfth century, and the same is proved for *Narcissus*. Thus, of the translations of Classical works mentioned in the well-known passages of the *Flamenca,* all those which we can date approximately are prior to the last quarter of the twelfth century . . . Is it probable that *Piramus and Thisbé* is from this thirty year period in the twelfth century which saw arise in Anglo-Norman territory a whole series of translations of Classical works, one of the least of which is the *Roman de Troie?*[23]

A few of the dates and facts in this quotation could be re-
vised, but the essence of De Boer's remarks is undoubtedly correct.

V *Romance Form*

Edmond Faral has said that the romance was invented when
someone thought to put into octosyllabic rhymed couplets, in
vernacular French, the contents of a Latin art epic.[4] We venture
to guess that the individual who did this was a vassal of Thibaut
de Blois, perhaps at Meun-sur-Loire. Ancient Latin poetry was
taught admirably at Meun, and one of the most distinguished
medieval Latin poets in France had been trained there by Hubert
de Meun. We are referring to Baudri de Bourgueil, who for
years was abbot of Bourgueil (Indre-et-Loire)—which was down
the Loire from Meun—and later became bishop of Dol (Ille-et-
Villaine) in Normandy.

This Baudri de Bourgueil lived half a century earlier than
the beginnings of the romance form; but his influence was
strongly felt in the Loire area, and he was doubtless typical. Phyllis Abrams, who edited his poems, says of him:

Baudri is a true precursor of the poets of the end of the twelfth
century . . . one can already note the school methods . . . and
even in certain of his poems an affection for analysis, monologue
and description. In form and in spirit, Baudri is a precursor of an
entire movement in literature in the French tongue at the close of
the twelfth century.[5]

He wrote, among other things, an imaginary exchange of poems
between the poet Ovid and a friend Florus. Ovid is writing
from his exile on the Black Sea and Florus desires to be with
him. Florus says (in words composed by Baudri): You have
not taught the world about love . . . the world has taught you
. . . the god [Eros] made our nature full of love; nature informs us that the god taught this . . . you were the narrator
not the inventor of love . . . May the comic poet perish, and
also the tragic, if the mild breeze from your pages is ever destroyed. . . . Ovid answers this and urges the pseudo-Florus

to remain in Rome, saying that Pyramus and Thisbé were more fortunate than he (Ovid). Ovid feels himself growing very weak. These imagined lines are filled with actual quotations from Ovid's poems. Baudri died in Préaux (Seine-Inferieur) in 1130.

Granted that there was this active imitation of the ancients prevalent in western France, particularly in territory occupied by subjects of the English king, and granted also that the form of the Anglo-Norman rhymed chronicles contributed by giving a vehicle to this adaptation of Latin art epics, there was something else—very important—which manifested itself in twelfth-century France, and made absolutely necessary the creation of the romance. This was a subjective spirit which was coming into men's minds—and hearts. It is not easy to explain and define this new "tenderness"; but it is essential that the student should know that it was there. If these next few pages are somewhat difficult to read, we suggest that the reader pass them over, and just remember that a wave of emotionalism—call it Romanticism, if you will—pervaded men's thoughts at this moment in history. It was to last a long time.

VI Romantic Spirit

This new spirit of pity, tenderness, and inner manifestation of love began with St. Anselm in the latter half of the eleventh century and culminated in the teachings of the Franciscans in the thirteenth century.[6] Its progress is evident in the theologians: St. Anselm of Canterbury, St. Bernard of Clairvaux, and later in St. Francis himself—but it is manifested also in the secular world, in the transition from Epic to Romance. The spirit of the Epic—the Carolingian spirit—is dominated not by imagination so much as by collective effort and heroism; in the Romance, on the contrary, there predominates the quest of Carnal Love seeking its spiritual object—the search of the individual. The ideal of mass Endurance gives way to yearning on the part of the individual pilgrim, to a logic of Will. The idea of heroic human life dissolves before Romanticism. In the twelfth century the Cistercians, followers of St. Bernard, were central in this doctrine. As R. W. Southern expresses it:

[Chrétien's] romances are the secular counterpart to the piety of Cîteaux. Of both love is the theme. Love is an inward thing, and therefore a lonely thing united only to its unique object. So the knight of Chrétien's romances seeks solitude for the exercise of his essential virtue . . . The twelfth century saw the creating of a new popular literature which carried far and wide the conceptions of love and devotion developed in their different ways by St. Bernard and Chrétien de Troyes. The views which reached the popular ear were less disciplined and exacting than those we have hitherto examined, but the community of feeling cannot be mistaken . . . It was not until the twelfth century that the imagery of journeying became a popular expression of spiritual quest.[7]

The theology that lies behind this change can be briefly sketched. Before St. Anselm, it was held that Man was saved from the consequences of sin because he had voluntarily withdrawn his feudal allegiance from God and given it to the Devil. God could break this new relationship only by forcing the Devil to violate the feudal rules. The Devil did not recognize at first the Divinity in Christ made Flesh. He attempted to force the Son of Man, who owed him no allegiance, to break with God, His true Lord. In this way the empire of the Devil was dissolved. By the new doctrine of St. Anselm Man had sinned and could be redeemed only by Man—by God become Man. This new theology aroused in the thought of the twelfth century a fuller appreciation of the suffering of the Redeemer.

The new concern with Love, both divine and human, spread rapidly in the twelfth century.[8] The mystic Richard of St. Victor (d. 1173), in his treatise on the *Four Stages of Violent Charity*, speaks of the love that wounds (first stage), the love that binds (second stage), the love that is absolute and unique (third stage), and the love that is for ever insatiable (fourth stage):

> In the first degree . . . God enters the soul, and the soul returns to itself. In the second it ascends above itself and is raised to God. In the third the soul . . . passes entirely into God. In the fourth . . . it descends below itself . . . it goes out by compassion. (*P.L.*, Vol. CXCVI, cols. 1217c-d)

Another mystic, St. Hildegard of Bingen (1098–1170), was convinced of the unity of human and divine love:

> It is God who gives being to a man's love in the form of a woman . . . The beloved is the source of perfection for her lover, and at the same time he can attain and bring to perfection the fountain of

Sapientia (Divine wisdom), the fountain of utter joy, which she embodies for him. (*P.L.*, Vol. CXCVII, col. 167b)

In this "new" preoccupation with the definition of Love in the twelfth century, the great problem was the relation between divine and human love. Soon this began to be examined in the light of Aristotle's terminology: the passive intellect and the active intellect (*De Anima* iii. 5) within the soul. Eventually the active was associated with the lover and the passive with the beloved. St. Bernard's closest friend, Guillaume de Saint-Thierry (1085–1148), identified Love and Intellect. The Neoplatonic concept of the Divine Mind and the World Soul were brought into this. The World Soul was identified with the principle of life, and with Sapientia. Some of the philosophers were haunted by the idea of divine marriage—such as that of the Divine Mind with the World Soul. This was even one of the interpretations given to the Song of Songs of the Bible. It must not be forgotten that St. Bernard was particularly concerned with the Song of Songs and wrote seventy-three sermons on this expression of Divine love.

The reader will see in some of this a foreshadowing of the thirteenth-century doctrine of the *dolce stil nuovo* in Italy. For the twelfth-century clerical world, at large, the so-called divine marriage could find its earthly counterpart in physical union. We close these remarks with a reference to the Cistercian Gérard de Liége (mid-thirteenth century), who composed three works on love. He claimed that the virtues gained by the soul illuminated by Divine Grace were to be compared with those of the lover when his soul is irradiated by his lady's grace. He asserted that the love poets had borrowed from St. Augustine and other Church Fathers.

VII *Alberic's* Alexander

We have suggested that the Anglo-Norman rhymed chronicle helped in the making of the romance form. A link between the rhymed chronicle and the true romance is in the *Alexander* fragment of Alberic de "Besinzo," which was adapted into Middle High German by the Bavarian priest Lamprecht about 1130.[9] The earliest version of this German poem is in the Vorau manuscript of the mid-twelfth century. A more elaborate version dates from around 1170, in a Strasbourg manuscript.

Alberic wrote in Franco-Provençal, vulgarizing in all probability a Latin popular chronicle which was in turn dependent upon the Archpriest Leo's *Historia de preliis* and the Julius Valerius chronicle. Of Alberic's poem, there are preserved only 105 lines; but we can estimate something of the rest from the 1,533 lines of the Vorau German version. These contain the birth of Alexander, the acquiring of Bucephalus, the arming of Alexander, Philip's death, Alexander's beginning to reign, his expeditions to Italy, Africa, Egypt, Syria, and Tyrus, Darius' letter, and Alexander's reply.

The Alberic fragment was discovered in 1852 in Cod. 35. Plut. LXIV of the Laurentian Library in Florence. The Vorau manuscript of the German adaptation is embellished a little, for the 105 preserved lines of Alberic are equal to 200 lines in the German text. It is quite evident that Romance-speaking minstrels were reciting songs about Alexander the Great *before* Alberic's work, for Alberic states:

> Some of the troubadours say that the king was the son of an enchanter. These wicked slanderers lie, and you will be unfortunate to believe even one of them, since he was of the lineage of an emperor and son of the king of Macedonia. (vss. 27–32)

When the romance form came into full blossom in the 1150's there was a strong influence in style and technique from Vergil's *Aeneid*.[10]

We have said that writers such as Chrétien de Troyes and Marie de France were perhaps growing tired of "Romantic talk" about the ancients in the current trend of the 1150's—the so-called *matière de Rome*. In his *Cligés*, Chrétien writes:

> Our books have taught us this that Greece was the first to have reputation for knighthood and learning. Then knighthood and the best of learning came to Rome, and now it is arrived in France. May God grant that it be kept there and that it will like the place so that never will there go from France the honor that has been there. God had given it to the others, but of the Greeks and Romans one does not speak any more. Their fame has gone out, and the living coal is extinguished. (vss. 30 ff.)

Chrétien obviously wants to talk about "modern" people: the later Byzantines and the folk of Arthur's court. In other words, he is instituting a new genre within the romance form. Marie de France (see p. 15 above) says much the same thing. She had thought of translating from the Latin, but so many others had done so, by which she means *too* many. Perhaps we might put it this way: the ancient East was now turning towards the West.

The current prominence of the English king and the Byzantine emperor went far to influence the choice of new material made by Chrétien and Marie. Both desired to free themselves a little from the ancient background which prevailed around them, and which they felt was stifling artistic creativity, but at the same time they attested the existence of this imitation of Classical antiquity.

The greatest contribution made by Chrétien (or possibly by an obscure predecessor)[11] was to put into the new romance form a body of legends which were later referred to as the *matière de Bretagne*. This is the setting of King Arthur's court and the knights of the Round Table. We will sketch the development of this Arthurian material.

VIII *King Arthur*

An individual whom we call Gildas wrote (*ca.* 540) a lament on the fall of Britain to the Anglo-Saxons. This is known as the *De excidio et conquestu Britanniae ac flebili castigatione in reges, principes, et sacerdotes, episcopos.* He mentions there the siege of Badon Hill, which, he says, took place in the year he was born—presumably shortly before 500. This "Badbury" was somewhere within the modern counties of Wiltshire—Berkshire—Dorset. The chronicler Nennius, who wrote his *Historia Brittonum* in the ninth century, devotes Chapter LVI to a chieftain Arthur ("Artorius") who won twelve battles—the last being at Badon Hill, where this Arthur himself slew 960 men. It can be assumed that Nennius was using a Welsh poem which gave a panegyric on Arthur. A Welsh elegy, which we call *Gododdin*, by the sixth-century Welsh poet Aneirin, mentions in vss. 1241–2 that "a certain chieftain fed black ravens on the wall of the city, although he was not Arthur."

On the basis of these bits of evidence it is assumed that there was an actual Welsh chieftain named Arthur. It is entirely possible that this leader fought the Picts in Strathclyde (Lake District and Dumfrieshire) and the English in Northumbria. This Arthur is mentioned again in the *Annales Cambriae;* he is found in the Welsh Book of Taliesin, in the Black Book, in the *Culhwch and Olwen,* and in the *Spoils of Annwfn.* The Triads in a Welsh manuscript known as the *Red Book* are gnomic aphorisms of groups of three, Possibly those triads which mention the *llys Arthur* (court of Arthur) date from as early as the eleventh century. Herman of Laon says that nine canons from his city, while journeying from Exeter to Bodmin in Cornwall, were shown a chair and an oven belonging to King Arthur, "famed in the fables of the Britanni." Apparently even at this early date there was a current belief that Arthur would someday return to restore the power of the Welsh. His grave (Avalon?) was not yet revealed.

By 1125 William of Malmesbury, in his *History of the English Kings,* proclaimed that in the *nugae Britonum* ("trifles of the Britons") they are raving about Arthur (see Chambers, p. 250) who is not worth dreaming about in false fables and yet is mentioned in serious histories as having supported his countrymen in war. Geoffrey of Monmouth claimed to have obtained material for his *History of the Kings of Britain* (*ca.* 1136) from a fellow master named Walter. Geoffrey was a master at Oxford in 1129 and he died as bishop of St. Asaph in 1154. He says of his source:

Whilst I was thinking upon such matter [kings of Britain], Walter, Archdeacon of Oxford, a man learned not only in the art of eloquence, but in the histories of foreign lands, offered me a certain most ancient book in the British Language that set forth the doings of them all in due succession.

Speculation as to the genuineness of this book in Celtic has been rife; but the book itself has never been identified. In 1154–55, Wace, a professional poet from the Isle of Jersey, adapted Geoffrey's history into Old French verse. This is called the *Brut.*

It is there that he added the existence of the famous Round Table (vss. 9994 ff., and 10555, 13675). No one knows his source for this.

Chrétien's method of selection from this material cannot be determined with any precision—except that he quite surely used Wace, and probably Geoffrey. He may have been acquainted with oral tales as well. It is possible that he had other written materials which are now lost.

IX Contents of Chrétien Manuscripts

We close this chapter with an examination of the two principal manuscripts that have preserved Chrétien's romances. They will give some idea of the "company" which his poems kept in thirteenth-century libraries. Collective manuscripts, particularly in the thirteenth and fourteenth centuries, were put together on order from wealthy patrons. They indicate what such a patron was reading. We are particularly impressed by the presence of Calendre's *Histoire des Empereors de Rome*. This was composed in lower Lorraine early in the thirteenth century. It claims to have been taken from a favorite chronicle of the Byzantine emperor. The name *Calendre* does not look very French.

The romances of Chrétien (not including the *Guillaume d'Angleterre* and the *Philomena*) are preserved for us variously in some eleven manuscripts. Two of these have special importance for the understanding of Chrétien's work and the rise of the romance form. They are Bibliothèque Nationale 794, usually designated as A, and the Bibliothèque Nationale 1450, commonly referred to as F. We will list the contents of these two manuscripts:

In MS A
  folios
    1–27 *Erec et Enide*
   27–54 *Lancelot*
   54–79 *Cligés*

   79–105 *Yvain*
   361–94 Chrétien's *Perceval*
Works other than Chrétien's in this same manuscript are: folios
   106–82 *Atys et Profilias* by Alexandre de Bernay
   184–296 *Roman de Troie* of Benoit de Sainte-Maure
   286–342 Wace's *Brut*
   342–60 Calendre's *Histoire des Empereors de Rome*
   394–430 First Anonymous Continuation of Chrétien's *Perceval*
   430–33 The Continuation which we ascribe to Wauchier de
           Denain
This manuscript was copied after 1215 and is in the Champenois
dialect. The patron for whom this collection was made was interested primarily in Chrétien, and it would seem likely that
he joined these poems with what he considered useful background material: the *Brut* and certain *matériaux antiques*. The
scribe's name was Guiot.
   The other manuscript (F) contains:

Folios
   1–83   *Roman de Troie*
   83–112 *Roman d'Eneas*
   112–39 Wace's *Brut* (first part)
   140–58 *Erec et Enide*
   158–84 *Perceval*
   184–88 First Anonymous Continuation of *Perceval*
   188–207 *Cligés*
   207–18 *Yvain*
   221–25 *Lancelot*
   225–38 Remainder of Wace's *Brut*
   238–64 *Roman de Dolopathos*
This manuscript is also from the early part of the thirteenth
century. The dialect has a trace of Picard.

CHAPTER 3

The Early Works

Aт the beginning of his *Cligés* (vss. 1–7), Chrétien lists his earlier works. We have already commented upon these and have identified the *Commandemanz Ovide* as Ovid's *Remedy for Love;* the *Art d'Amors* we accept as Ovid's *Art of Love.* The *Mors de l'Espaule* must refer to the myth in which Pelops was served to the gods as food by Tantalus, his own father, who wished to prove that the gods were not omniscient. This last tale is mentioned only briefly in Ovid's *Metamorphoses* (vi. 401–11). The tale of Mark and blond Iseut is, of course, a Tristan narrative; the transformation of the nightingale, the hoopoe, and the swallow is the "Philomela" tale in *Metamorphoses* vi. 412–676. We can only guess that these adaptations are listed in chronological order rather than to suit the rhyme.[1]

I Remedy for Love

The *Remedy for Love* was probably quite amusing to young people in Chrétien's time and place. Marie de France in her *Guigemar* (vss. 229–44) describes the living apartment of the young lady whom Guigemar was to love. The lady's elderly husband, quite rightly, did not trust her.

The lord of the town had constructed a chamber inside the wall of his castle to keep his wife secure. Right at the entrance was a chapel. The chamber had painted walls; Venus was well represented there and she showed the details and the condition whereby a man could preserve love and be a loyal and good lover. But Ovid's book in which he confides how anyone can get rid of love—Venus is shown throwing this into a fire and she is excommunicating all those who would read that book or follow its teaching.

We have no hint of how Chrétien handled this material found in the *Remedy for Love,* nor do we have a similar adaptation by any other medieval poet. In the absence of this we must assume that Chrétien remained faithful to the original, as is likely in the case of a novice poet. The Latin original has 814 lines, so we can judge that Chrétien's treatment was little more than that length. Here is a summary:

The God of Love upbraids the poet for choosing such a subject. Ovid responds that love can be cruel and a murderer and that Eros should let the hapless victim have some hope for escape. The god of love replies, "Do what you will." This advice is for women as well as for men. If they had only listened to Ovid, many wretches might have been saved: Phyllis, Dido, Medea, Tereus, Pasiphae, Phaedra, Paris and Helen, the Trojan people, the daughter of Nisus, Myrrha, Philoctetes. One should begin the cure early while there is still a chance. Idleness is a great breeder of love. Go off to battle, put your idle mind to work. (Marie de France may have had this in mind when she said, "If anyone wishes to avoid vice he should study and begin some heavy task; in this way he can get farther away and free himself from great pain" [Prologue, vss. 23–27].) A place in the country is a help. Drive the tamed bulls to plough, plant seeds, and pick fruit. Do routine duties. One can also hunt and fish. It is well to travel far off and never look behind (Marie's *Eliduc* lost love for his wife in this way). Stay away as long as the fire is there.

There is no use to take potions or seek charms. Have no faith in spells. Try to see the loved one in a bad light. She or he may have been false. (In Marie's *Bisclavret* the lady loses all her love when she knows her man is a werewolf.) Look at the ugly things about her person. She is too tall, fat, or thin. If she cannot sing, ask her to do so. If her teeth are crooked, get her to smile. If her eyes are watery, persuade her to weep. If she waddles, get her to take a long walk with you. It might be well to visit her early before she puts on her makeup. In the act of love see how poorly she responds. Do not call me obscene for giving this advice. You might try another lady shortly before and then make comparisons. When you are quite fatigued from making love, notice any body blemishes that she may have. It might be well to have two sweethearts at the same time. (In the *Chaitivel* of Marie de France, the lady had four lovers and this made her unable to love *one*, when he alone survived.) If you want to win another lady, read Ovid's books on the *Art of Love*. You have only to play hard to get and one will come running. Always have in reserve some girl that you can have easily.

You might try excess. See too much of the lady and you will soon be fed up. As long as you are jealous, love will endure. Cupid told Ovid that if a man keeps thinking of his troubles love will not last. Keep away from lonely places and live in the midst of people. (In Chrétien's romances it is suggested that a knight who follows the tourneys may fall out of love.) Do not keep company with other lovers. When you break off with your former loved one do this cleanly, and make it plain. (Laudine breaks with Yvain very positively.) Remember, however, that you must always have some kindliness for a person that you once loved. Never become hostile. If you are bitter in your denunciation you can easily fall in love again. The need for a clean break is very necessary. Do not give the discarded one a chance to correct her faults. Have a look at more beautiful ladies. Above all, do not read old love letters. Wanton loves are fed by wealth and power on the part of the woman (Perhaps Guenevere would not have looked about if she had been poor.) Dancing and poetry will keep you from breaking off your affair. Do not be jealous of another man who gets the lady after you. When you can embrace your rival you are cured. Some foods should be avoided. Too much or too little wine will help you lose your love. Those who drink moderately are the most ardent lovers.

In the course of this résumé we have mentioned some episodes

from Marie de France and from Chrétien's work where the
Remedia may have been in mind. It is our contention that the
Remedia had a most active influence on the writers of these
romances—even more than the *Art of Love* itself. The *Remedia*
was shorter and more to the point. It is likely that Chrétien
began his literary career with this adaptation.

We will continue with this survey, giving some idea of the
probable content of Chrétien's other formative works that have
not survived.

II   The Art of Love

Ovid's *Ars amatoria*, the likely original of the poem Chrétien
identifies as the "Art d'Amors," is divided into three books.
The first tells how a man can acquire love (772 lines); the
second gives advice for retaining love (746 lines); the third
contains advice for the woman (812 lines). Here is a summary:

Book I. First find a girl that you can really love. Look for
her everywhere. The race track is an excellent place, because
you have to sit close there. Dinner parties and watering places
also make fine "hunting" places. Make excuses for touching her.
Men cannot pretend well; women are able to hide their desires.
Gain the confidence of the lady's attendant; she will talk about
you as she dresses her mistress, but will not give away your
secret once she has come to know you. The lady may seek
to persuade you to buy something for her. Resist this. Write
her letters, promising a lot. If she returns them unread, keep
trying. Follow her about, but not too closely. Be careful not
to overdress; but keep yourself clean: wear clean toga and good
sandals, keep your hair properly trimmed and your nails clean
and short, and have a pleasant breath. At the table, trace mes-
sages with your finger dipped in wine, gaze into her eyes, drink
from the rim where she has drunk, touch her hand. Get her
husband to like you and let him talk freely, but drink not too
deeply yourself. Sing or dance if you can. After the dinner, draw
close and flatter her. Pretend you wish to be "just a friend." Do
not be shy about making promises. Let her see tears on your
face. It will help if you are very pale. Once you have had

a kiss the rest will come soon. Do not wait until she makes the first passes at you. Do not speak of her to your best friend; he will cut you out. The method of attack will depend upon the kind of lady.

Book II. You should not resort to charms or love filters. Beauty soon fades. Get culture and speak two great languages well. Be tolerant and tactful. A wife likes to quarrel, but a mistress must not be crossed. The husband has a legal right; you have only love on your side. Of course, a rich man gives big presents and needs no help from Ovid. A poor man must proceed with care. Do not mind if the lady is a little rude; she will become kinder. If she keeps resisting, yield a bit. Agree with all she does and says. When you play games with her, let her win. Do not be ashamed to wait upon her. Come running when she wants you. Use your wits to get near her. Give presents to her servants; send her fruit, or a thrush or a dove. Be cautious about sending her poems. If you do, be certain she is praised in them. If you have promised freedom to a slave, give it in her name. Praise the way she dresses and looks. If she becomes ill, show devotion but do not importune her. Hang around and let her get used to you—no long journeys. You need not stick to this one woman, but be very discreet. If she does find out about the other woman, be nonchalant. Prove with her in the bed that you could love no one else. Eat foods that stimulate love. Perhaps you should then tell her about the other girl. She may get violent, but if you embrace her for a while she will soon soften for everything. Above all, "You must know yourself." Put your best foot forward. That is Apollo's advice. But do not read your own poetry aloud! You will have to have patience. Do not trouble her when there is another man on the hook. Let her deceive. Only the husband should try to trap lovers. When you make love to her, do it secretly and in darkness. Do not find flaws in her person or in her nature. You will get used to these. Do not ask her age An older woman is more experienced and often more delightful. After thirty years women know more. Do not make love in a hurry.

Book III. Women should have fun while they can. Improve your beauty as much as possible. Modern taste demands cultivation. Who cares about the "Old Rome" where everything was ugly and coarse! Ovid is glad he is "modern." The modern age has developed culture, taste, and manners. You do not need heavy jewels and gold: just be elegant. Dress your hair to fit your type of face; dye your hair in old age and buy wigs near the temple of the Muses. You need no fancy clothes; just choose the proper color. Keep free from odor, shave your legs, wash your teeth twice a day and your face in the morning. Use the proper kind of cosmetics and do not leave the boxes visible on your dresser. Procedures ugly to watch can have lovely effects. Pretend you are sleeping when you apply cosmetics. Men can watch you comb and brush. Beautiful girls require no aids; but such are few. Try to hide your bodily defects. If you have but little hair, keep this a secret. If your bust is too flat try bandages. Eat a few lozenges if your breath is bad. When your teeth are blackened, do not smile. Learn to control laughter; do not bray like an ass. Show dimples and teeth in a smile. Do not strike your thighs and wiggle when you are amused. You should learn how to weep nicely. Mispronounce a little if you wish; some will think this charming. When you walk abroad be moderate in carriage. Your shoulders should be bare because they are charming. Sing when you can and play the tune upon a lyre. Read the poets with a practiced voice—soft and low. Dancing is very good and you should know some simple games. By these you always win in the end. Be a good loser. Do not engage in active athletics, but walk a lot. Go to the theaters, the public spectacles, and the races. Display yourself in public and you will find the right lover. Do not trust a man who dresses too fancily, for he is surely a deceiver. Beware of the philanderers. But do not accept gifts if you are not intending to give your favors. When a man writes you a note, send a maid for it and read it with care. Try to make out whether he means what he says. Do not keep him waiting too long for your reply. Do not yield at once, and do not refuse. Let your reply be written by a slave. Be sure that all previous writing on the wax has been erased. Make it seem to anyone reading your letter that it has been sent to another woman.

Do not show anger, pride, or glumness in your face. Be the life of the party, for Romans like gaiety. Expect from each man what he is best able to give. Treat the old experienced fellow differently than you would a boy. But do not make admittance too easy for anyone. Let him think he is not the only one. It is not hard to deceive a husband. Even if you have many guards around you there are nonetheless ways. (Marie says this in her *Milon*.) A friend can carry out a wax tablet under her arm; you can write a message in milk on a friend's back. There are temples and there are baths; one can also visit a sick friend. A guard can be deceived by wine, by drugs, or by having a maid to sleep with. You can use a bribe. Do not trust other women; they will steal your man. Your maid should not be too pretty. Eat daintily. Too much food is much worse than too much wine; but do not let the wine go to your head. In the final act of love, lie on the couch in a way that makes you seem attractive. Pretend at least that you share with him the culmination of love.

This summary is important, for it shows the reader to what extent Chrétien and other writers of romance were indebted to Ovid for many of their descriptions and comments. Indeed, the instructions of the god of love in the *Roman de la Rose*, which many find most enjoyable reading, are based closely upon these given by Ovid. But although Ovid had written all of this more than eleven hundred years before, the material was thoroughly absorbed by our twelfth- and thirteenth-century poets, and we can be quite sure that this was active advice to medieval young men and women, just as much as it was to those who lived in the time of Caesar Augustus. It was thoroughly assimilated, although the principles of hygiene expressed therein were not rigorously practiced in the twelfth century.

Chrétien necessarily knew his Ovid very well, particularly because of his adaptations; but he has considerable independence in his writing. On the contrary, his contemporary, Marie de France, was more in debt to Ovid, even for small details. She was, after all, deemed an expert on love by the knights and ladies of her day, and her chief model could only have been Ovid. In our opinion, not much of the detail in her *Lais* was owed to the Breton tales that she had heard in her youth. One should look rather to Ovid as her principal source.

III *Pelops' Story*

We should like to say that the young Chrétien found the entire source for his story of the "Shoulder-bite" in the *Metamor-*

phoses; but the treatment of the theme there is indefinite and not sufficient to inspire an independent poem. This is what Ovid gives:

> When such tales had been told the people immediately came back to the present and lamented Amphion who had died with his children. Their mother was to blame. Pelops is said to have wept for her; after he had removed the clothing from his breast he showed her a left shoulder of ivory. At the time of his birth this shoulder was of flesh and of the same color as the right one. Soon thereafter, when his limbs had been cut up by his father's hands, they say the gods joined them together, and when the other pieces had been found there was still lacking the place between the collar bone and the top of the arm. An ivory piece was inserted for the part missing, and when this had been done Pelops was whole again. (*Metamorphoses* vi. 401–11)

It was undoubtedly from this passage that Chrétien got the suggestion for writing his story, because this is in *Metamorphoses* vi., 401–11, and the "Philomela" tale which he treated follows directly after (vi. 412–74). Since Chrétien surely knew no Greek, the only place where he could have read the remainder of the Pelops story was in Hyginus' *Fables* 82, 83, 84, and 85.[2] These fables are very brief summaries. From these he would have learned that Tantalus, the father of Pelops, was a son of Jove who was invited to his father's table on Mount Olympus. He was false and transmitted the secrets of the gods to men. Finally he decided to test the omniscience of the gods; he cut into pieces his own son, Pelops, and fed them as food to the gods. Only Ceres was deceived. She ate a bit of the shoulder. When she learned the truth she brought the boy to life again and supplied the missing piece in ivory. Tantalus was sent to Hades, where he stands in water with apples above his head, unable to drink or eat.

Hyginus gives more on Pelops. Pelops looked for a bride. The daughter of Oenomaus, Hippodamia, was very beautiful. In order to win her, a lover had to defeat her father in a chariot race. The horses of Oenomaus and his golden chariot were supposedly unbeatable and the price of defeat was death. Pelops bribed Myrtilus, the charioteer of Oenomaus, and thus won the race. He did not keep his promise to Myrtilus. In later years, Chrysippus, an illegitimate son of Pelops, was kidnapped by Laius. Pelops recovered his son but his wife Hippodamia was jealous. She had the boy killed by her sons Atreus and Thyestes. When Pelops blamed her for this, she committed suicide.

This entire narrative may have been treated by Chrétien. It is quite similar in "goriness" to the *Philomela*. The problem remains, how did he get a copy of Hyginus? There was a ninth century manuscript which has since disappeared. Fortunately, the text was printed in 1535, at Basel, by a man named Micyllus. This is the only extensive version that we have. A few additional manuscript fragments have been found. Manitius[3] believes that Richard de Fournival knew a copy of the full manuscript. It gives some insight into Chrétien's character to realize that he gained access to what must have been a rare manuscript even in his day.

IV   The Tristan

The mention of the early narrative "Del roi Marc et d'Iseut la Blonde" faces us with the tremendous problem of the early versions of the Tristan romance. Did Chrétien write a complete Tristan story, or just a Tristan episode? Was his version the first narration of the complete story in the Old French language— what we commonly refer to as the *Ur-Tristan*? The earliest *Tristan* which we have (partially extant) is the Thomas *Tristan,* in Anglo-Norman, which, it is believed, was composed between 1155 (date of Wace's *Brut*) and Chrétien's *Cligés*—perhaps we should date this about 1160. Gaston Paris insisted that Chrétien's poem was only an episode; Wendelin Foerster believed it was the complete story.[4]

No one can write with complete assurance on this matter. We will state our belief. Most scholars agree that the first suggestion of the Tristan plot came from southwest Scotland, across the Solway to Carlisle, from the land of the Picts and Scots. The name Tristan may be a derivative of Trest, a Pictish name. Possibly the primitive tale was an account of how a vassal steals the wife of his overlord— Motif R 225.[5] The early Tristan may have been a swineherd of King Mark's, to judge by the

Welsh Triads. Certain crude episodes in the version of the twelfth century could be remnants of the earliest narrative. For example, the episode in which Iseut sent her attendant Brangwyn off to the forest to be killed, and afterwards is remorseful when the would-be killers free her. Other such episodes are the one in which Iseut is won from Mark by an Irish minstrel—and won back, of course, by Tristan; and, still later the one in which the guilty Iseut is turned over to the lepers by Mark, and is once again saved by Tristan. These episodes seem rude and primitive. Also, Tristan is said to be from Loonois (Lothian), and he and Iseut go to dwell in the forest of Morois (Moray), and these names suggest a Picto-Scottish origin.

Presumably the tale was carried southward through what is today the Lake District—Cumberlandshire and Westmoreland-shire—and reached Cornwall and Wales. We will guess that some form of it was soon put into French in that area. This would be the *Ur-Tristan*. Chrétien doubtless drew upon this for his own narrative. This was his first attempt at what we now call the *matière de Bretagne;* and from this effort came his later interest in Arthur and his knights. It is usual for scholars to date the *Ur-Tristan*, whatever its detailed contents, in the 1150's. We are assuming that Chrétien first encountered this material when he was visiting in England, probably at Glastonbury.

V   *Breri and La Chiévre*

Many problems remain about the Tristan story—in fact, this subject is "all" problems. Most of these have no special bearing on the matter of Chrétien's version. Thomas, in his *Tristan,* refers to Breri as an authority on British history:

Lords, this tale has many variants, and for that reason I bring it together in my verses and retell what is necessary, leaving aside the rest. I do not wish to overdo this unification: the subject matter differs here. Among those who are used to telling and narrating the Tristan story, they tell it differently, as I have heard from many people. I know what each one says and that which they have written. But from what I have heard they do not follow Breri who knew the doings and the accounts of all the kings, of all the counts who have been in Britain. (Douce Fragment, vss. 835–51)[6]

This must be the Bledhericus about whom Gerald the Welshman says:

> . . . on which occasion that famous dealer in fables, Bledhericus, who lived a little before our time, mysteriously said: "There is amongst us a people who, when they go out in search of prey, carry their horses on their backs in the place of plunder; in order to catch their prey they leap upon these horses, and when it is taken, they carry their horses home again upon their shoulders." (*Description of Wales*, chap. viii)[7]

In the First Continuation of Chrétien's *Perceval* (vs. 13945) there is a knight named Bleheri. In the *Meriadeuc* the father of the protagonist is Bleheri, sire des Vaus de Blanquemore et du Lac as Jumeles (vss. 6826, 7306).

This Bledhericus should be taken seriously. There must have been some narrator of tales about Britain who bore this name. As he obviously produced what Thomas considered an important version of the *Tristan*, it is entirely possible that his account was what we think of today as the *Ur-Tristan*. This would have been Chrétien's primary source.

There is also the problem of La Chiévre. The *Roman de Renart* (Branch I b, vss. 1 ff.) begins:

> Lords, you have heard many a tale which many a narrator has told you—how Paris stole Helen and the pain and trouble he had from this—about Tristan which La Chiévre composed, who spoke quite well . . .

We have mentioned this in our Chapter I, along with the variant name Li Kievre. We cannot explain La Chiévre any more than we can identify Bledhericus.

VI   *The* Philomena *and Crestien li Gois*

We must now consider "*Et de la hupe et de l'aronde Et del rossignol la muance . . .*" This means unquestionably that Chrétien had composed a version of the "Philomela" tale, adapting this from Ovid's *Metamorphoses* vi. vss. 411–674.

It has been mentioned in our opening chapter that Gaston Paris, and others, identify this with an extant version of the *Philomena* (1,468 vss.) which had been inserted into a large compilation known as the *Ovide Moralisé*, dating from about 1307. The compiler of this *Ovide Moralisé* says that he had included the Pyranus and Thisbé *"si comme uns autres l'a ditte"* and also this *Philomena* "si com Crestiens le reconte." This reference to Crestien without further qualification makes me quite convinced that the poem in question is the work of our famous Crestien, namely Chrétien de Troyes.

An intriguing complication here is that the Crestien in question says of himself (vs. 734): *"Ce conte Crestiiens li Gois."* Cornelis de Boer and Gaston Paris were certain that "li Gois" was an early name of Chrétien de Troyes. Wendelin Foerster did not agree, and Raphael Levy has been very vigorously opposed.[8] There have been various explanations for "Gois." The word "goy" is used among the Jews for "Gentile," and, in many instances, designates specifically, a Jew who has become a Christian. Crestiens li Gois could mean, therefore, "Chrétien the former Jew." Those who do not wish to accept that Chrétien could have been a convert—and these are many—are obliged to interpret this appellative differently, or to deny that this *Philomena* was the work of our poet. Raphael Levy interprets "li Gois" by a different Jewish word, refusing to believe that this author could be Chrétien de Troyes. We now give a résumé of Crestien li Gois' Old French version.

Pandion of Athens gave his older daughter Progne to King Tereus of Thrace. No cleric was at the wedding; there sang under the chamber all night the long-eared owl (*dus*), the tawny owl (*huanz*), the cuckoo, the barn owl (*fresaie*), and the raven. The Furies flew into the room. Later this couple has a son, Ithis; when he is five years old, Progne yearns to see her sister Philomena (Ovid has Philomela). Tereus goes to Athens to fetch her and while there falls in love with Philomena. Here Chrétien adds a minute description of her beauty such as was in vogue in twelfth century romances. Also, she is said to be skilled in hunting, and in such games as draughts, chess, the "old game," and *bufe* and *hamee*. She knew the authors and grammar; could read the Psalter, and could play the *gigue* and the *rote*. (Ovid has no such description of beauty and talent.) Chrétien blames

Amors for this improper attachment. There is much pleading between Tereus and Pandion. Finally, Philomena is allowed to go. On landing, Tereus takes her to a ruined house (*maison gaste*) in a wood. (At this point Chrétien names himself as Crestiiens li Gois.) Tereus begs for her love. She calls him wicked (*fel de put'eire*), etc. He cuts off more than half her tongue, leaves an old woman with her who knows how to weave and spin, and goes to Progne and says her sister is dead. She is crushed with grief and sacrifices to the "devil Pluto." In the meantime, Philomena manages to weave a "cortine" (wall hanging) without interference from the old woman. She looks out the window and sees the city where her sister lives. She persuades the old woman to carry the "cortine" to the queen. Progne understands at once and follows the woman on her return, without being seen. She breaks in the door and leads her sister away to a lower chamber in her palace. (In Ovid, Progne slips out during a Bacchic procession and brings home her sister in Bacchic disguise.)

Progne sees her little son pass by. Her devil (Pluto) advises her to murder him. She softens under the child's embrace, but then she hardens again and, because of the Devil, cuts off his head while he is in her arms. The two sisters cook the flesh. Progne invites her husband to come to feast on what he likes best. After he has eaten a little, he goes and asks for Ithis. She tells him he has eaten his son. Then Philomena throws the bloody head in his face. He chases them with a sword and is turned into a filthy hoopoe, while Progne becomes a swallow and Philomena a nightingale. Philomena is, of course, anxious that all false lovers and ravishers shall be destroyed, so in early spring the nightingale cries throughout the woods "oci, oci," that is, "kill, kill."

Crétien has retained the principal elements of Ovid's narrative, but he adds details in conversation and description that suit twelfth-century tastes.

VII *The Lyrics*

We have now discussed all the early works known definitely to have preceded the *Erec*. But Chrétien is also the earliest

lyric poet in Old French whom we know by name. Two extant
lyrics are attributed to him, and we must say something about
these. The first occurs in *chansonnier* manuscripts U and C.
In the margin of U a later hand has written that this poem
belongs to Chrétien. This is No. 121 in Raynaud's *Bibliographie
des chansonniers.*[9] It consists of six stanzas with an envoi of
four lines. We cite the first stanza and then follow with a translation of the whole.

> Amors tançon et bataille
> Vers son champion a prise,
> Qui por li tant se travaille,
> Qu'a desresnier sa franchise
> A tote s'antante mise,
> S'est droiz qu'a Merci li vaille:
> Mes ele tant ne le prise
> Que de s'aie li chaille.

Love [designated by "she"] has undertaken contest and battle
against her champion who toils for her so much that he has put
all his intent on justifying her privilege—and it is right that she help
him with Mercy, but she does not think enough of him to care to
help him.

Whoever attacks me for Love's sake I am ready without reward
and without deceit to go into combat for her, for I have well learned
the torments; but I fear that when I serve her she may lose the
war. I do not wish to be so free in any way that she not keep a
lien on me.

No one, if he is not genteel, can learn anything from Love; but
such is her custom, from which no one can appeal, that she desires
to sell entrance privileges and free passage, and she must dispense
with Reason and put a limit on rewards.

A silly heart, inconstant and flighty, can learn nothing of Love.
But my heart is not like that for it serves without expecting Mercy.
Before I thought of getting caught I was harsh and savage toward
her. Now I like, without telling any reason, to suffer because of her.

Love has sold me dear her prestige and her power over me, for
at the outset I have dispensed with Moderation and given up Reason.
Their advice and their aid may never be returned to me. I lack
their company and they can expect nothing from me.

I know of no escape from Love nor can anyone tell me of one.
My plumage can moult in her coop all my life, but my heart will
not moult (change) at all. I have my intent on Love so that I am

afraid she may kill me; but for that my heart does not change. If Mercy does not help me, and Pity which is lost, the war will end which I have maintained so long.

The second of these poems is found in twelve chansonniers: T, a, R, H, C, U, V, L, N, K, P, X. In Ms P there are two slightly differing versions. The best version seems to be in T, a, and R, which offer the text that Foerster and Bartsch-Wiese have preferred. This poem is No. 1664 in Raynaud. Chrétien is mentioned as the author of this poem in C, R, T, and a.

There are six stanzas of nine verses each. We give the first stanza in the original.

> D'Amors, qui m'a tolu a moi
> n'a soi ne me viaut retenir,
> me plaing einsi qu'adés otroi
> que de moi face son pleisir;
> et si ne me repuis tenir
> que ne m'an plaingne, et di por quoi:
> car çaus qui la traïssent voi
> sovant a lor joie venir,
> et j'i fail par ma bone foi.

About Love who has taken me from myself and does not wish to retain me for herself, do I complain, and at the same time I grant that she may follow her pleasure with me. I can never keep from complaining and I will tell you why. I often see those who betray Love achieving joy, and I cannot do so by displaying good faith.

If Love wishes to win over her enemies to exalt her power, that is sensible, I believe, for she cannot betray her own people. I, who cannot leave her whom I supplicate, I send to her my heart which is hers; but I do not imagine I do her a favor when I render to her what I owe her.

Lady, since I am your man, tell me if you are grateful for this. No, if I ever understood you, you are sorry that you have me. Since you do not desire me I am yours contrary to your pleasure. But if you ever should have mercy upon someone, please suffer me, for I cannot serve anyone else.

I never drank of that potion by which Tristan was poisoned, but a true heart and good will makes love better than he. I should be better received because I was never forced in any way, except that

I did believe my eyes, and therefore am I on this path from which I shall never go astray, nor have I ever been weary.

Heart, if my lady does not hold you dear, you must never leave because of this; you must always be in her power since you have undertaken this. Never, according to my advice, will you have enough of Love, but do not be dismayed when times are hard. A good thing is sweeter because of delay, and the more you will desire her the sweeter she will be when you have her.

I would find Mercy, I am sure, if she were throughout the whole world where I seek her, but I believe she is not there. Never do I cease, never do I tire of beseeching my sweet lady. I beg and beg again like one who cannot flatter or serve Love without sincerity.

These two poems do not offer original thoughts; but perhaps they were demanded by circumstances and were not just "poetry." In the first, Chrétien is desirous of fighting for Love but she does not seem to care. Of course, Love is very demanding, but he will never cease to love to the bitter end, despite Reason and Moderation. In the second, a lady is actually being addressed. The poet sees many being rewarded who are not true lovers, but he bestows his heart upon Love, which is not really a true gift because it belongs to Love already. He wants to know whether the lady appreciates him. After all, he has loved of his own will, not, like Tristan, because of a potion. He wants his heart to remain always in her possession. One should not mind too much difficult times, because the gift is all the sweeter when it must be long awaited. He would like to search for her everywhere. As it is, he begs her over and over, and this is sincere —not mere flattery.

These lyrics by Chrétien show influence in both form and matter from Bernart de Ventadorn and other Provençal troubadours. It is difficult to pin this down precisely; but this is certainly the impression received. Bernart de Ventadorn makes constant use of six, seven, or eight stanzas followed by an envoi. Take, for comparison of subject matter, the poem of Bernart's which begins "*Lo rossinhols s'esbaudeja. . . .*" In the second stanza we read: He gets more from Love who courts with pride and with deceit than he who begs all day long and humbles himself too much; For hardly does Love desire one who is "franc" and loyal, as I am. She [Love] has taken from me all my happiness, because I have not been false and treacherous. In the envoi we find, "Tristan, even though it may not be evident to you, I love you more than one is wont to do."[10] Here is a stanza from Raimbaut d'Aurenga's *"Assatz sai d'amor ben parlar. . . ."* The first stanza is as follows:

I know how to speak very well of Love for other lovers; but for my own benefit, which is dear to me, I can say nothing and tell nothing; for to me there is no use for wealth, praise nor curses nor bitter words; for without success am I now towards Love true and good and *franc* and loyal.[11]

We cannot tell when Chrétien wrote these two poems, but, as already suggested, they probably were composed in his earlier years.

CHAPTER 4

The Erec and Enide

I<small>N</small> the edition of the *Erec and Enide* first published by Wendelin Foerster in 1890 there are 6,958 lines; the version published by Mario Roques from the Guiot manuscript (B. N. fr. 794) has 6,878 lines. The poem is found in these manuscripts: B. N. 375, 794, 1376, 1420, 1450, and 24403; Chantilly (Musée Condé) 472. Fragments have been discovered in the Annonay manuscript,[1] in a Mons manuscript,[2] in Bibliothéque Ste-Geneviéve 1269, and in the Laigle fragment.[3]

We have every reason to assume that this poem was the earliest Arthurian romance composed by Chrétien, excepting the lost Tristan romance or episode, and therefore, as this poem represents the launching of a new genre, we should expect to find evidence of experimentation. It seems certain that at the time Chrétien was acquainted with various *chansons de geste*, with the antique romances *Thébes, Eneas,* and *Troie*—and with some poem about Alexander. He also knew, of course, the Tristan material, troubadour love poetry, and most certainly Wace's *Brut*.[4]

Hofer has dated this *Erec* in 1171; Fourrier, followed by many others, sets it as late as 1176.[5] In our own opinion, the correct dating is in the 1160's. This would better suit the comparative chronology. Bezzola is among those who agree that the *Erec* was written for Henry II of England and Eleanor of Aquitaine. We would not go so far as this. We believe, however, that it was done in England, under the influence of Glastonbury and of the Winchester entourage of Bishop Henry of Blois.

More specifically, we suggest that the young Chrétien drew his Arthurian setting from legendary material circulating in southwestern England and from Wace's *Brut*.[6] He may have drawn the first suggestion of his plot theme from the *Roman d'Eneas,* where an individual knight serves as protagonist and reacts to courtly society as he found it. This pattern is persistent in the *Erec*, the *Guillaume d'Angleterre*, the *Yvain*, and the *Conte dou Graal*. William S. Woods has stated this well:

A hero achieves the realization of his worldly ambitions and desires [at the beginning of the narrative]. He then becomes aware of some fault, error, or less obvious reason, which forces him to abandon his lofty pinnacle of happiness. This point serves to motivate the main body of the poem which is a series of adventures concerned with the hero's effort to recover his former status, presumably through his becoming more deserving of it, by the correction of his error or by the expiation of his fault.[7]

We will say further that Chrétien's typical procedure was to portray a "purifying" Quest. The *Lancelot* also belongs to this grouping. A protagonist achieves a certain goal or quest, fighting his way through difficulties—often supernatural. He is purified by surmounting the difficulties—sometimes his purity is never lost and he is merely tested through his adventures.

Such individual adventures, presented with care . . . in Chrétien's time, could well have had symbolic meaning (there are, however, some scholars who doubt this). No problem is posed by the presence of Celtic themes among these trials; but it is our contention that when such themes were used it was because they suited Chrétien's general thesis. We do not believe that Chrétien put together a chance hodgepodge of stories in a rambling folkloristic way, with no special sequence of motifs. Chrétien makes clear his procedure at the beginning of the *Erec:*

The peasant says in his proverb that one often scorns a thing which is worth more than one thinks. For this reason one should examine a good thing whatever it might be. If such study is neglected something may be passed over which could prove to be most enjoyable. For this reason Crestien de Troies says it is right that every one should be intent upon learning and then retelling; [Crestien] makes out of an adventure tale a very fair composition [*conjointure*] which shows that it is not right to do nothing with what is known, as long as God gives the grace to do it. This tale is about Erec, the son of Lac, a narrative which professional minstrels are accustomed to breaking up and ruining before kings and counts. (vss. 1–22)

In plain language, this means that Chrétien had heard the basic plot of the *Erec et Enide* recited by professional minstrels and that he felt this catchy tale could be improved by embellishing its plot (*matière*) with some meaning (*sens*), thus, with the grace of God, making a fine *conjointure*[8] or union of *matière* and *sens*. Certainly this is an indication that the poet took a simple narrative (perhaps full of Celtic themes) and, by adding meaning, made a fine thing out of it.

It is most regrettable that today we cannot interpret the inner sense of this narrative sequence in a way that may be acceptable to all scholars. We can only restate our opinion that this *Erec* was carefully designed. At the same time we agree that it was up-to-date for its age, conforming to popular tastes at the courts in England and Champagne, and illustrating psychological nuances which pleased the knights and ladies of around 1160–70 —and had appeal for the bourgeois class as well. In the *Erec* there are guilt feelings and "communication" troubles between Erec and Enide shortly after their marriage. Erec's feeling that he must be on the defensive disappears only after the seventh of his adventures undertaken with Enide at his side.

I   *Résumé of Plot of* Erec et Enide

One springtime morning, while holding his court at Cardigan, Arthur decides to hunt the White Stag. Gawain objects, and reminds the King that he who kills the stag must kiss the fairest lady of the court, which would arouse dissension, for each knight will suggest his own lady. Arthur, nevertheless, begins the hunt the following day. Queen Guenevere lags behind with one of her ladies-in waiting, and with Erec, the son of King Lac and a knight of the Round Table. In a clearing the three see a knight accompanied by a maiden and a dwarf. The queen wishes to meet him, but the dwarf resists the approaches of her lady-in-waiting and of Erec, who then swears to arm himself and challenge the knight. The king, having killed the stag in the meantime, takes counsel to determine which lady he will kiss, and at the queen's suggestion it is agreed to postpone a decision until Erec returns from his encounter with the unknown knight.

Erec sets out and follows the knight into the fortified town of Lalut, where he takes lodging with an impoverished vavassor (a knight of lesser rank). This vavassor informs him that on the following day there is to be a celebration, and for this reason many knights are assembled. The terms of the day are that the bravest knight's lady may lift a sparrow-hawk from its silver perch. For the past two years the knight whom Erec followed into town had won, and if he triumphs unchallenged again this year he will have permanent possession of the bird. Erec at once resolves to make a try for the hawk on behalf of the vavassor's beautiful daughter. The following day he defeats the knight, Yder, and would have killed him had he not begged for mercy. Erec receives Yder's pledge to put himself, his lady, and his dwarf in the service of Guenevere. True to his promise, Yder appears in submission before the queen, and at Arthur's urging he is forgiven and made a member of the court.

Meanwhile Erec passes an agreeable evening at Lalut. The next day he and his lady set off alone for Arthur's court, she riding a gift palfrey and carrying her hawk, he obviously in love. At Cardigan, Erec presents his lady to Guenevere. He explains that she is the daughter of a poor vavassor, but that she is of noble birth since her mother was the sister of the local count. She comes clad in poor linen only because Erec had refused the offer of an ermine and silk robe from her cousin, preferring to have the queen herself outfit his lady. Guenevere praises him for this, and garbs her in a rich tunic, a mantle, and a fine gold belt. She is presented before the assembled Round Table; and Arthur, with the consent of all his court, gives her the kiss of the White Stag.

At the feast of Pentecost Erec weds his lady, and learns her name to be Enide. That night their marriage is consummated under the blessings of bishops and archbishops, and the celebration continues for a full fortnight. The court determines to have a tournament to end the festivities; the knights assemble in the plain below Benebroc a month after Pentecost. Erec and Gawain both distinguish themselves, but all present agree that to the former must go the glories of the tournament. Arthur is pleased with the performance of Erec, whom he now holds second in esteem to his nephew Gawain, and grants Erec's request to quit the court and take the new wife to his father's kingdom.

On the fifth day of travel they arrive at King Lac's residence at Carnant in Wales, where they are received with great pomp and festivity. Compelled by tender love for Enide, Erec forgets the tournaments and settles into a routine which seldom takes him from his wife's side. This complacency sets the other knights to talking. Enide is ashamed to hear that they look upon Erec as a coward and recreant, and Erec overhears her one morning lamenting the cause of her sorrow. He determines to set forth without delay, taking only his wife for company, although his father wishes to provide him with an escort in accord with his social position. Enide recognizes the foolishness of her grief, but bravely accepts the consequence of her hasty words. As they depart, Erec warns Enide not to speak to him unless he should address her first, but when three robbers approach from the rear, Enide cannot restrain a cry. Erec turns to the attack, dispatches them one by one, then warns Enide again that she is not to speak without his leave. Leading the three captured horses, they advance not a league before five more robbers threaten. Enide again cannot prevent a cry, and Erec chastises her for lacking trust in him and not respecting his command. After forgiving her a second time he spurs into the fight and easily defeats the five, taking their mounts as prizes.

The following noon they meet a squire carrying food to certain field laborers, and he gladly shares it with them. Erec rewards him with a choice horse, and the squire rides ahead to the town to have lodging prepared for them. Although they are well received, the local count is jealous of the handsome young knight, and wishes, moreover, to steal his beautiful wife. The unsuspecting Erec gives the count leave to speak with Enide, and she seems to succumb to his promises of a rich and happy life. She suggests that the count carry her off the following day, and kill Erec when he attempts to pursue them. Early the next morning, though, Enide warns Erec of the plot and they hastily quit the town, leaving their captured horses as payment to their host. The count recognizes the deception and gives chase. Once more Enide cannot hold back a warning cry, and Erec vows to punish her lack of esteem. He turns to face the count and his hundred knights, and kills one of them before wounding the count himself. The other knights wish to pursue Erec, but the count acknowledges his guilt and restrains them.

Erec and Enide pass through a meadow and arrive at a walled place with a drawbridge, which they cross. The lord of the place, Guivrez li Petiz (whose men are Irish), rides forth to defend his lands, and Enide again warns her husband of the impending attack. After a hard battle Guivrez submits to Erec, and promises henceforth to aid in any trouble that may befall him.

Although badly wounded, Erec rides on until he arrives at the edge of a large forest where Arthur has come to hunt. Kay, in a playful spirit, puts on Gawain's arms. He meets Erec without recognizing him, and invites him to rest and have his wounds treated at Arthur's camp. Erec replies harshly that he prefers not to quit his road, and then unseats Kay, who returns and relates the adventure to the king. Now Gawain is sent to induce the unknown knight and his lady to join Arthur. When Erec again refuses, Gawain cleverly detains him while the camp is shifted on the road. Erec, realizing he has been tricked, reveals his identity and agrees to stay.

The next morning Erec and Enide leave precipitously. Before long they hear a girl lamenting her knight (Cardoc de Tariol), who has been carried off by two giants. Erec rushes to his rescue, kills the two giants, and sends the grateful knight to Arthur. In his haste to return to his wife Erec causes his wounds to reopen; he falls in a faint, bleeding, from his horse. Enide believes him dead, and wishes to kill herself for having induced him to pursue these adventures. Her hand is stayed by a passing count, Oringle de Limors, who wishes to wed the beauteous lady. Bringing the body of Erec, they go to Limors. Oringle forces Enide to marry him—but he cannot force her to be happy. Erec recovers from his faint to see her resisting the advances of the count. Oringle's men flee, believing he is a devil (ghost). He kills Oringle and flees with his wife.

Meanwhile, word has come to Guivrez of a knight, found dead in the forest, whose lady was forced to marry Count Oringle. He suspects this knight is his friend Erec, and together with a thousand men he sets out to kill the count and rescue Enide. That night he encounters the escaping Erec, and, unable to recognize his wounded friend in the darkness, defeats him. When he discovers Erec's identity, Guivrez begs forgiveness, and they pass the night there in the woods. The following day they arrive at Penevric, where they remain until Erec's wounds are healed. Afterwards, in the company of Guivrez, Erec and Enide set off for Arthur's court.

They arrive the first evening at the fortified town of Brandigant, where Erec wishes to spend the night. Guivrez, however, warns him that no one leaves alive who seeks the town's adventure, which is called "Joy of the Court" (*Joie de la cour*). Nonetheless, Erec enters the town and, against the advice of every one, goes into the magic garden where flowers and birds sing in wonderful abundance. He sees there a row of stakes, each supporting the head of a knight who had lost his life seeking the Joy (one stake, prepared for Erec's head, has only a horn upon it). Erec goes on until he sees a comely maiden. As he approaches her, he is challenged by her knight, whom he defeats. This knight, who calls himself Mabonagrain, then tells how he had been tricked by his lady into promising he would not leave the garden until some knight should defeat him and blow the horn, for thus she hoped to keep him by her side. Erec then sounds the horn and all rejoice, except the lady, who fears to lose her knight. Enide comes to comfort her, and they discover that they are cousins. All are happy, and the Joy continues for three days. On the fourth day Erec departs with his wife and Guivrez for Arthur's court at Robais, where they arrive amid great elation nine days later.

Erec remains there until the death of his father, King Lac. He then goes to Nantes in Brittany where, at Christmastide, he is crowned by Arthur himself before the assembled Round Table. Enide is reunited with her parents, and everyone in Nantes, noble and commoner alike, celebrates the succession with appropriate splendor.

II *Discussion of Plot*

Chrétien was aware that his new tale was running a bit long, for he says: "It would be hard for me to say it again, for this story is not a short one" (vss. 6425–26); "but I will not tell it to you again, becasue one who tells something for a second time adds to the boredom of his narrative" (vss. 6272–74); "when I do not list for you the various dishes which they were served I am being reasonable; I must be intent upon something else" (vss. 6875–78). It is evident that he was not certain how such a lengthy tale would be received. He must have been reassured, however, for most of his later romances run about the same length, nearly 7,000 lines.

We assume that Chrétien added to his source story a considerable amount of ordinary embellishment, as contrasted with symbolic meaning. There is some humor, although this is difficult to prove in a romance composed eight hundred years ago. A typical example is the prank perpetrated by Kay, which turns out ill for him. Gawain has left his horse saddled and ready, tied to a *charme* ("hornbeam") tree. Kay rides off with it, and then, feeling important and believing he will not be recognized, tries to force Erec and Enide to come with him to Arthur's court. Erec and Enide both recognize Kay; but he does not know them. (Enide hides her face with her wimple.) Kay is, of course, unhorsed, and he has to admit the horse is not his. Also, the idea of a group of "brave" men running away from a devil is funny for many people. Erec recovers consciousness and slays the knight who is annoying his wife. The knight's followers had thought him dead; they now believe him to be a ghost (a *deable*). "One after another they run away—with big leaps as fast as they can. Going out of the hall they all cry, weak as well as strong, 'Run, run, see the dead man.' There is a pile up at the door" (vss. 4815–73).[9]

This romance is not dedicated to a patron. Bezzola suggested that it was written for Henry II and Eleanor of Aquitaine, but we disagree. The romance form, of course, was copied from the antique romances which preceded it. We have proposed that Chrétien used the *Eneas*. The basic content of the *Eneas* is repeated in the *Erec* in verses 5290–98. Another echo is in *Erec*, verse 6391.[10]

Roger Sherman Loomis proposes a Celtic origin for the episode of the Sparrow Hawk prize.[11] This episode, of course, may have been in the original adventure tale which Chrétien improved. Other suggestions have been that the White Stag may reflect a pagan ritual, and that the Hunting of the White Stag and the name Guigomar come from Marie de France's *Guigemar*.[12] On the other hand, we are not so sure that this lay preceded Chrétien's *Erec and Enide*. It is our belief that Chrétien used William of Malmesbury's *De antiquitate Glastoniensis ecclesiae*.[13] From this Chrétien may have derived the episode of the giants (vss. 4253 ff.), and the character of Yder, son of Nut, in the Sparrow Hawk episode. We have already stated that use was made of *chansons de geste* (see vss. 661–718 and Tiebauz li Esclavons, vs. 5727). Fernaguz (vs. 5729) is a name used (later ?) in the *Chevalier au Cygne*.

III *Names in the Romance*

Since the *Erec et Enide* was Chrétien's early venture into the genre of Arthurian romance, it was necessary for the poet to establish a *dramatis personae*. Some of his characters came, to be sure, from Wace and from Geoffrey of Monmouth: Arthur, Guenevere, Kay, Gawain, Merlin, Bedouer, *et al.* But there are many names which we cannot trace with any certainty. R. S. Loomis was convinced that many of these were distortions of Celtic names. This may be true; but such identifications must be approached with caution.[14]

If it is true that Chrétien was in the Glastonbury region when he wrote this early romance, he would have found Welsh names close at hand. The Welsh word *llan* denotes the enclosed land of a church—and another word, *lan*, the softened mutation of *glan*, can signify "holy" or "saint." It is probable that Lancelot, first found here in the *Erec*—and the Lanval in Marie's lay of that name—are to be associated with such a *lan*. The silly champion of the *Joie de la Cort* episode (vss. 5319–6074) is called Mabonagrain. It can be assumed that the first syllable here is Welsh *mab* or *map* meaning "son." One cannot pin down the interpretation of Brandigan, name of the castle where the *Joie de la Cort* takes place, but it looks Celtic. The literature that has been written on the name Guigemar or Guigomar is very extensive. It is assumed by many that this was taken from a Celtic tale. Stefan Hofer insists that the name was "forged" by Chrétien himself;[15] but he agrees that these Celtic elements were the basis of the name: *gwyn* "white" and *mar* "great." The name Guigomar in early British speech would have been Uinnoc-moros. Perhaps this was the name of some primitive hero who was celebrated in British-speaking territory. What we are opposed to, and perhaps Hofer is too, is the assumption that Chrétien, in selecting such a name, had before him a vast network of Irish and British legendary material. Some characters who are mentioned in the same context with Guigomar in the *Erec* appear to have names drawn from the edge of a *Mappa Mundi* (medieval world map).

In this romance Chrétien introduced for the first time Lancelot del Lac (vs. 1674), Perceval le Gallois (vs. 5106), Sagremor le Desreé (vss. 1701, 2175, etc.), Yvain (vs. 1685), Morgant la fee (vs. 1907), and Enide. His central list is the one presenting the names of the knights of the Round Table: these are Gauvain, Erec, Lancelot del Lac, Gornemanz de Goort, Biax Coarz, Les Hardiz, Melianz des Liz, Mauduiz li Sage, Dodin le Sauvage, Gaudeluz, Yvain le Preu and Yvain l'avoutre, Tristant, Blioberis, Caradué Briebraz, Caveron de Roberdic, son of King Quenedic, the vassal of Quintareus, Ydier del Mont Delereus, Galeriet, Quez d' Estraus, Amauguin, Galet le Chaut, Gilflet, Taulas, Loholz, Sagremor le Desreé, Bedeoir, Bravain, Lot, and Galegantin le Galois (vss. 1671 ff.). There are thirty-one knights in this compilation. Some of these characters were destined to be developed by Chrétien in later romances, notably Lancelot, Gauvain, and Yvain; others are repeated only occasionally, chiefly in the *Conte dou Graal;* still others are never mentioned again.

The two names that we wish most to identify are Erec and Enide. It was our opinion, for a time, that Erec was Scandinavian; but the Norse writers in their derivatives of this romance do not seem to identify it as such. The Norse render Erec by Erex, which would suggest that this name was strange to them also. Customarily in early Welsh material a chieftain is addressed as

Eneit "soul." This makes one wonder wether Chrétien could have known this fact and transferred the use of *Eneit* "soul" into a term of address for a lady. One name in the romance is definitely Welsh: this is Caradué Briebraz, which is, beyond question, *Caradoc breich braz* "Caradoc of the good arm." Finally, as Erec and Enide approach the Castle of Cardigan the important members of the Arthur's court, mounted on high places, watch them arrive. Those who watch (vss. 1501 ff.) include Guenevere, Kay, Gauvain, Cort the son of Arés (never mentioned again), Lucant the butler, and Perceval. Could the name Perceval have been derived at this time from the verb *percevoir*? Probably Chrétien did not plan at this stage to promote him to a major protagonist.

Another significant list is that giving the names of the guests at the wedding feast of Erec and Enide. These are Bransle de Colescestre, Menagormon sire of Eglimon, the count of Traverain, the count of Godegrains, Moloas sire of the *Isle Noire* ("black Island"), Greslemuef de Fine Posterne (= *Finibus Terrae*) and brother Guingomar who was lord of the Isle of Avalon and lover of Morgant the Fairy. There came also David of Tintajuel, King Garrat of Cork, King Aguiflet of Quirion, and the old king of Orcel. Finally there were the two dwarfs Bliant and Bilis, kings of the Antipodes, with two of their vassals, Gribalo and Glodoalan (vss. 1871 ff.). The reader will understand now why we have suggested that Chrétien in his wide search for additional names may have made use of the outer edge of a *Mappa Mundi.*

IV *Beginning of this Romance*

R. W. Southern says:
Chrétien probes the heart, but it is the enamelled heart of the twelfth-century secular world; not yet made tender by the penetration of strong religious feeling. There is nothing in Chrétien like the passage of the *Morte d'Arthur* when Guenevere takes leave of Lancelot.[16] This, of course, is true of the Chrétien of the early romances—but not of the later Chrétien who wrote about the Grail. We now give our own account of how the *Erec and Enide* could have come into being. Young Chrétien, while

in the entourage of Henry of Blois, abbot of Glastonbury and bishop of Winchester, read the history of the Abbey composed by William of Malmesbury. Chrétien already knew some stories about Arthur and his knights which were circulating at Glastonbury and near the Celtic border. He thought of making use of these in the new Romance form—being tired, we suggest—of the flavor of the already existing antique romances. (His two extant lyrics indicate that he was already imbued with the troubadoresque concept of a "perfect lady"—the *Amor* celebrated there.)

Yder the son of Nut was the principal character of an Arthurian tale which had been incorporated into William of Malmesbury's history. Chrétien wanted a better knight to contrast with Yder. For some reason not known to us he named him Erec. This Erec is maltreated by Yder's dwarf and snubbed by Yder; but Erec established the fact in the Sparrow Hawk contest that his lady (*eneit* "lady") was the fairest of all. Chrétien did not wish to stop his romance at this point; so he continued with the idea that she was also the most faithful of all. Chrétien imagined a series of dreadful trials. With a faithful heart Enide braves her husband's anger and keeps by his side, warning him.

Such an explanation of the genesis of the Erec and Enide leads from a troubadour concept of love into a higher one, such as was cultivated by the court at Champagne. The trials which are undergone seem to have a progression. Perhaps they represent the Cistercian idea of spiritual progress which was prevailing so strongly in certain circles. Chrétien, as we have noted, began to be afraid that his narrative was too long. Obviously the public for whom this romance was intended was not adversely critical, and the new Arthurian romance, as regards length and characters, was soon firmly established.[17]

V *Comparison with the* Yvain

It is possible to assume that Chrétien later, in his *Yvain,* was especially influenced by this *Erec and Enide.*[18] In both of these romances the protagonist's first adventure is the performance of an exploit which King Arthur had intended to accomplish himself with full court. (We propose that this motif came from the Yder story in the history of Glastonbury Abbey.) In both

cases Arthur is rather inferior to Guenevere and the hero or
protagonist meets a strange individual—a wild man, or a dwarf,
and both have the motif of the Hospitable Host with his beautiful daughter. Both heroes oppose the proprietary interest of
some champion and defeat him. They are reunited with Arthur's
court and there is a marriage. Perhaps the narrative should end
at this point, for the pinnacle of happiness has been reached,
but in each romance there then begins a new series of adventures; either further proof of prowess is required, or the hero
sets out to work off his guilt. At this stage of the story both
Erec and Yvain have *nine* more separate adventures. Whenever
the protagonist is successful he seeks Arthur's court; when he
is remorseful he stays away. Both protagonists are healed by
ointment provided by Morgant the fairy. In both the *Erec* and
the *Yvain* the last four adventures of the series of nine appear
to be superfluous. The story might well have ended after the
fifth. In each case this final group of adventures begins with
a fight with giants (or a giant). Enide watches over Erec at
night; the lion does this for Yvain. Erec's combat with Guivrez
and Yvain's with Gawain are bitter fights between good friends,
followed by reconciliations. Perhaps the *Joie de la Cour* episode
in the *Erec* is parallelled in a way by the *Chastel de la Pesme
Avanture* in *Yvain*.

VI *Adaptations*

Towards the close of the twelfth century, Hartmann von Aue,
a South German from the Black Forest region, began to imitate
Chrétien's romances. He adapted the *Erec and Enide,* and some
ten years later composed his own *Iwein*. His *Erec* is less polished
than the other. The *Erex Saga,* in Norse, was adapted at the
close of the thirteenth century. In this nearly all the proper
names are different. The *Geraint Son of Erbin,* found in the
Welsh *White Book* (thirteenth century) is probably freely imitated
from Chrétien's *Erec*. Apparently the Welsh name Geraint came
from Latin *gerontius*. The *gerontea* is the medicinal herb
"groundsell," called in French *seneçon*. Aside from its association
with old age nothing further can be said about it.

CHAPTER 5

The Cliges

I<small>N</small> vss. 8 ff. of this romance Chrétien de Troyes remarks that he:

> . . . begins a fresh tale about a youth who, in Greece, belonged to the lineage of King Arthur, but before anything· is said of him you will have an account of his father—when he came and from what family. [The father] was so valiant and of so brave a heart that he went from Greece into England, which was then called Brittany, in order to acquire fame and reputation. We found this story, which I am about to tell, written in one of the books in a chest in the Cathedral of Saint Peter at Beauvais. The romance was taken from this by Crestien. The book is very old, which is evidence that the story is true, and can be believed all the more. Through the books that we have we come to know more of the doings of people in olden times.

This romance has 6,784 lines in the Foerster edition, and 6,664 lines in that published by Mario Roques. It is preserved in eight manuscripts: Paris B. N. frc. 1374 (S), 794 (A), 375 (P), 12560 (C), 1420 (R), 1450 (B), and a manuscript of Turin, no. L. I 13 (T).[1] The well-known Annonay manuscript, already mentioned, has a fragment, and there are other fragments at Tours, Oxford, and Florence. The B. N. 794 is the Guiot manuscript used as the base of the Mario Roques edition.

Because the poet lists, at the beginning of the *Cligés,* only the *Tristan,* the *Erec and Enide,* and the Ovidian adaptations, it is generally assumed that this romance was composed directly after the *Erec and Enide.* The *Cligés* is quite different. The *Erec* used only Arthurian materials, whereas the *Cligés* is a combination of Byzantine and Arthurian romance. We have mentioned earlier (pp. 28–9) an association of interests which existed between Champagne and Germany and the fact that Germany was pro-Byzantium. We assume that by the time Chrétien began work on this *Cligés* he had returned to the Champenois area. Before examining the settings and possible sources of the poem, we analyze the plot in some detail.

I *Résumé*

Alexander, the first-born of the emperor of Greece and Constantinople, comes with twelve companions to King Arthur's court in Britain, where he hopes to be made a knight by Arthur himself. True to his father's only request. Alexander shows himself exceedingly generous, and is heartily welcomed at Winchester, where he becomes a close friend of Gawain.

Having left his kingdom to the care of Count Angrés of Windsor, Arthur passes over into Brittany with his wife, her attendant Soredamors, and Alexander for company. On the ship the two young people fall in love, but Alexander dares not speak to the girl. Preferring to hide his feelings, he laments his state in a lengthy, allegorical monologue. Soredamors, for her part, also experiences this love, but fearful of appearing too bold, she can only express it to herself, and only in a similar way.

At the end of October, messengers come to tell Arthur of a revolt planned by Count Angrés. After assembling a formidable army in Brittany, Arthur returns to Britain, where he knights Alexander and his companions. The queen gives Alexander a fine silk shirt, into which Soredamors has woven one of her golden hairs to see if a knight can distinguish it from the pure gold thread. Thus knighted and equipped, Alexander sets out with Arthur's army to Windsor, where Angrés has retired after sacking London. On the first day Alexander and his twelve companions distinguish themselves, and bring back four captive traitors to the queen. Arthur surlily demands that they be handed over to his justice, and has them torn asunder before the town walls. Alexander is rewarded for his bravery with the best kingdom in Wales and the command of fifteen hundred troops. The battle rages inconclusively all that day, and at night Arthur determines to reward with a golden cup, set with precious stones, any knight who takes the town. That evening, Alexander, as is his custom, visits the queen, who has Soredamors tell him about the golden hair in his shirt; later, in the privacy of his bed, Alexander lies in amorous ecstasy before this token.

That night the traitors of Windsor plot to attack Arthur's camp while his knights are sleeping, but an early rising moon reveals their presence and they are routed by the loyal troops. Count Angrés, with seven companions, sneaks back toward Windsor, but is seen by Alexander. Having exchanged their arms for those of dead traitors, Alexander and thirty loyal men enter the town without difficulty. Once inside they kill untold numbers, and drive the last resisters and Angrés into the tower, where Alexander himself fells the count with a blow from his club. He then leads Angrés and the captives to Arthur, who presents him the golden cup. Alexander gives this to the reluctant Gawain; he would rather have the hand of Soredamors, which he still dares not request in person. He declares his intentions to the queen, who recognizes the mutual love and willingly arranges the wedding, which is celebrated that very day at Windsor.

From this union is born, a year afterwards, Cligés. Meanwhile, in Greece, the emperor, who is about to die, sends messengers to Britain to summon his lawful heir. En route the ship is sunk; the sole survivor is loyal to Alexander's younger brother Alis. This messenger returns to Greece, saying that the ship was wrecked on the return voyage and that Alexander is dead. This lie is believed, and Alis is crowned emperor. Alexander hears of this usurpation and sails with a mighty army to Athens, where the rich and eloquent Acorionde serves as his emissary. Alis assembles his counselors, who advise him to avoid open conflict with his brother, and he agrees to give Alexander the ruling power if he might retain the titulary rights. Alexander agrees on condition that Alis never marry, so that following his death Cligés may become emperor. Peace is arranged on these terms.

Sometime later Alexander dies, after having exhorted Cligés to go to the court of Arthur to test his prowess, and to challenge even Gawain if need be. Alis, troubled by evil counselors, is unable for long to resist marrying. With a chosen company (among them Cligés), he goes to Cologne to win the daughter of the emperor of Germany, who has been promised already to the duke of Saxony (Sessoigne). This fair maid, Fenice by name, falls in love with the handsome Cligés, who returns her unspoken passion.

Cligés defies and defeats the nephew of the duke of Saxony. Returning from this encounter he gives Fenice a tender glance, and she is overcome by love. She reveals the cause of her illness to her nurse, Thessala, who promises to prepare a potion which will preserve Fenice's virginity and ensure Cligés of his lawful succession. At the marriage feast, Alis unwarily accepts the potion from the hand of Cligés, and that night, and thereafter, he possesses Fenice only in his dreams.

As the company returns to Greece they are pursued and challenged by the Saxons. Cligés, lightly wounded by the duke's nephew, runs him through with his lance and in youthful haste enters the ambush prepared for the Greeks. He defeats a Saxon champion and takes his arms. In this guise Cligés rides toward the Saxon army, pursued by the Greeks, who think him dead. The Saxons believe their champion has won, but at the last minute Cligés shouts his defiance and reveals himself as leader of the Greeks. In the ensuing fight Cligés captures the white Arabian steed of the Saxon duke. Under cover of the battle twelve Saxons carry off Fenice. Cligés alone observes them. As he approaches on his Arabian horse, six ride toward him thinking to announce their success to their duke. When Cligés hears the name of his lady he kills all six, then pursues and attacks those who had stayed to guard Fenice, letting one alone escape to tell the duke of the prowess of Cligés.

He rides back with Fenice to the Greek encampment, still fearing to express his love in words. There he learns that the Saxon duke has issued a challenge to single combat to determine the battle and the fate of Fenice. The two meet and the duke, exhausted, yields to Cligés. The day won, the Greeks return to Constantinople with their new queen.

Cligés now remembers his promise to his father, and asks leave to go to the court of King Arthur. Alis reluctantly permits his departure, and Fenice contemplates his parting words: "her to whom I am completely"—does he truly love her, she asks herself, or is this mere flattery?

Cligés arrives in Britain, and learns there is to be a tournament. He has his followers secretly purchase for him four suits of armor: one black, one green, one red, and one white. He rides forth on the first day in black and defeats Sagremor le Desreé (the "mad"), then retires incognito. The second day, in green, he defeats Lancelot, and wins great honors before again disappearing. The third day, all in red, he defeats Perceval before vanishing. That night he puts on his white armor and hangs the others outside his tent so that everyone may see there was but a single victor on all three days. The next morning the still unknown champion shows himself to Gawain and is invited to come to the court. There Cligés reveals his identity. He stays with Arthur until the summer, but love then calls him back to Greece.

Cligés and Fenice at last declare their mutual love, and Fenice tells Cligés about the potion. They wish to live together, but to avoid scandal they resolve that Fenice shall feign death and be buried in a specially constructed coffin from which Cligés will rescue her. Thessala prepares another potion, while Cligés arranges for his serf Jehan to prepare the coffin and a hidden retreat. Fenice, after refusing to be examined by physicians, seems to die. Three traveling doctors from Salerno pass by and remember the wife· of King Solomon who had attempted the same ruse. They entreat Fenice, then torture her, but she will not speak. More than a thousand women attack and kill these three for their excessive cruelties. Fenice, soothed by a special balm, is placed in the coffin and is buried. Her thirty guardians soon slumber and that evening Jehan and Cligés take the body to the tower retreat. Once there Cligés, not realizing the effects of the potion, thinks her dead, but when she hears his sighs Fenice recovers. Some fifteen months later Fenice goes out into the garden of the tower where she often lies with her lover in the summer. One day they are discovered there asleep by Bertrand, whose sparrow-hawk (*esprevier*) has escaped and flown into the garden. Cligés wounds Bertrand, but the latter escapes to tell the emperor that he has seen the empress. Realizing their plight, the two lovers escape to Britain with the aid of Thessala. Jehan is arrested and threatened with death. He tells Alis about the potion and criticizes him for breaking his promise to Alexander and Cligés. Jehan warns the emperor that, should he be killed, Cligés would rightfully avenge him. Alis, angered by the deceit, orders his nephew found. The search is fruitless, however, and Alis soon dies of grief at not finding Cligés. King Arthur prepares an army to avenge Cligés, but before it sails Jehan brings the news of Alis' death to Britian. Cligés is proclaimed emperor, and rules happily with his mistress as his wife.

It is interesting to observe that in the quotation from the *Cligés* with which we began this chapter, Chrétien equates England with Brittany. In verses 23–24 he calls this *Cligés* a *romanz*, a term which may first have been suggested to him by its use in the *Roman d'Eneas*. Also, dialectical discussion of love and its symptoms is encountered for the first time in this poem.

II *Is the* Cligés *anti-Tristan?*

Proposed by Wendelin Foerster, and then adopted by many others including Gaston Paris, is the opinion that the *Cligés* was intended to be anti-Tristan.[2] In the *Tristan,* as we can judge from the scanty remains, the author begins with an account of the union of Rivalin and Blanchefleur, the parents of Tristan. In the *Cligés,* the first section narrates the love and marriage of Cligés' parents, Alexander of Byzantium and Soredamors, the sister of Gawain. In the Tristan legend the tragedy of the parents foreshadows the love misfortunes of their son; but in the *Cligés* the preliminary love story has no special bearing on what is to follow between Cligés and Fenice. This suggests that the Alexander-Soredamors story is an imitation of the episode which came first in the *Tristan.*

There are four direct references to Tristan in the *Cligés.* First (vss. 2799 ff.) we are informed that Cligés knew more about fencing and the use of the bow than Tristan ever did—and also more about birds and dogs. In verses 310–516, Fenice, the German princess, states that she would rather be torn limb from limb than permit men to speak of her and Cligés as they have done about Tristan and Iseut, in tales that are too shameful to repeat. Iseut's love was base, because her body belonged to two men even though her heart was possessed by only one. She refused her love to neither. In verses 5199 ff., Fenice explains that if she and Cligés truly love each other they will not be compared with Tristan and Iseut—for in that case their love would not be honorable. In verses 5232 ff., Cligés sketches to Fenice his plan that they should go away together to Britain. But, replies Fenice, in this case they would surely be spoken of as another Tristan and Iseut for no one would realize that Fenice in actual fact had never had marital relations with Emperor Alis.

These four hostile references to Tristan and Iseut, added to the fact that Alexander's relations with Soredamor were chastely limited to wooing and marriage, are the chief basis for the belief that Chrétien was intentionally writing an anti-Tristan when he developed the *Cligés*. This is not necessarily true. Chrétien says quite plainly that the moral tone of the Tristan story was reprehensible; but we can hardly accept that Chrétien's main purpose in the *Cligés* was to censure adulterous love. Despite Fenice's hesitation before having physical love with two different men, during the same period of time, such behavior would hardly have shocked the mores of people living in the twelfth century. Furthermore, Tristan was the man whom Iseut really loved—and she had given herself to him before she ever met Mark of Cornwall. (One might even argue technically that Iseut was not married validly to King Mark since she could not have made her marriage vows to him with genuine intent.)

Courtly Love taught that a woman should be true to the man whom she actually loved, regardless of the marriage vow. It is not an easy task to determine precisely why the Tristan story was unsavory to twelfth-centure individuals. Was it because Tristan and Iseut were concerned only with love of the moment, and not interested in repentance and salvation? Be this as it may, the example of Iseut was held to be a bad one. Chrétien seems to have shared this feeling; but it could not have been the principal reason for his composing the *Cligés*.

It is quite probable that when Chrétien refers to the immorality of the Tristan-Iseut relation he has in mind an earlier version of the story which was used by Béroul and Eilhart von Oberge. The more polite tone which prevails in the versions of Thomas and Gottfried von Strassburg came later. What *was* the tone of the early Tristan versions?

Alberto Varvaro's *Il Roman de Tristan di Beroul*[3] is not an easy book to read, but it attempts to provide some solution for our problem about the earliest Tristan narrative, generally called the lost *Ur-Tristan*. Varvaro holds that Béroul too was mirroring the earlier story. In his opinion, Béroul and his source were concerned with each scene independently. There was a string of loosely related episodes, and the intervals between were somewhat empty. The love filter (like the Fate of the Ancients) gave a first impulse to the guilty lovers—but afterwards they sinned with free will. Béroul, and his predecessor (?), wanted one thing only—to promote sympathy for the love suffering of the guilty pair. When Tristan decides to repent it is for *practical,* not religious, reasons. The wicked characters do the least suffering, and their fear of death is more powerful than their fear of consequences from sin. According to Varvaro the tone in Béroul, and therefore probably in the *Ur-Tristan,* is a mixture of comedy and seriousness, and there is even some parody of the courtly knight. Although Chrétien in the *Cligés* speaks ill of the love of Tristan and Iseut, some thirty Provençal troubadours refer sympathetically to the guilty pair. Perhaps they were familiar with Thomas, a more moral version.

We have admitted influence on the *Cligés* from the *Roman d'Eneas* and an early Tristan narrative. It is agreed also that the Nisus-Euryalus motif in Vergil's *Aeneid* influenced the Cligés episode where Alexander and Arthur's army are besieging Count Angrés at Windsor. There is undoubtedly much influence from Ovid, as Guyer pointed out long ago.

D. W. Robertson, in a recent article on Ovid and the *Cligés,* proposed that both Ovid and Chrétien were using mocking humor in their portrayal of these love relations. Chrétien was a satirist, not a "slightly immoral romantic sentimentalist."[4] This interpretation would require much reorientation of nearly everyone's opinion of Chrétien; we will not discuss it further here. Of course, Chrétien, like many others, was capable of humor; but he was also representative of his era. Some believe that there was a close relationship with the *Eracle* of Gautier d'Arras; but influence could have run the other way.

III *Sources*

The principal theme in the *Cligés* is also found in Shakespeare's *Romeo and Juliet:* the motif of stealing a girl away from her spouse (or family) by giving a drug that will enable her to feign death. The plan is for the lovers to be united after she is revived in the tomb. The oldest known version of this is a *Solomon and Marcolfus* tale in which this trick is practiced by one of Solomon's wives.[5] Could this *Solomon and Marcolfus* have been the story in Latin that Chrétien read at the cathedral library at Beauvais?

It happened that on a certain occasion a pagan king who was neighbor to King Solomon came to be his guest. He slept with one of Solomon's wives and agreed to take her away from her lord. Marcolfus, a sort of magician-prophet, observing the wickedness of this Ethiopian queen, told all to Solomon. Solomon was angry with Marcolfus at the time and rejected his words. Marcolfus said. "You do not belive me? You will hear and see marvels with pain in your heart."

The wife, in accordance with her promise made to the pagan, pretended she was sick and then played dead. Marcolfus recognized this trick and told King Solomon: "It is not safe to believe a woman. She has not been sick, but well; she is not dead but living." Solomon was again angry and retorted, "You lie, you good-for-nothing." "I do not lie. I will prove the truth of the matter," Marcofus replied. "How do you intend to prove it"? "Give me some lead," Marcolfus answered. Marcolfus then melted the lead in a fire and poured it onto the palm of the queen's hand. She seemed to feel no pain, nor did she move a limb. Marcolfus said, "I will prove this more certainly, you will see; but wait a little."

The queen was placed in her tomb, where her attendants, in accordance with her request, had made an opening for breathing. Solomon was disturbed by the apparent death of his wife and before sunset he withdrew to his chamber. In the twilight Marcolfus came to him secretly and said: "Rise up and you will see that your wife is alive, and I wish to prove this is true." Solomon went to the tomb, accompanied only by Marcolfus; the latter went up on top of the tomb making a noise like a bull, striking the earth from the sepulcher with his hands and feet. The lady, alive in the tomb, thought he was a bull and said, "Sthy, Sthy, Sthy," while the king listened. Marcolfus inquired, "Is not this true what I said?" Solomon replied, "You lie, idiot. The Devil seduces you, and me as well as you." Marcolfus replied, "Tomorrow you will see new wonders and you will believe that I am speaking the truth. Rise tomorrow and come to the tomb; you will not find her there."

The pagan king, coming in the night, carried the queen away. Solomon returned to the tomb the next morning but, of course, did not find her. He went back to his chamber and began to weep bitterly, saying: "Who will get me out of this misery? Miserable me!" Calling Marcolfus he said: "I am sorry that I offended you by not believing you. Now I beg of you, lift up my heart, that my sadness may cease, if at least you can help me in some way." Marcolfus, sensing that King Solomon was already weakening, said with elation: "Where are your ministers who were wont to flatter you, bringing you to despair, sadness, and weakness of heart? Why don't they remove you from your sadness and bring you to joyous times? But you never need Marcolfus." Solomon answered, "You will get what you want." Marcolfus replied, "Give me three troops of men, one in black, the second in red, and the third in white." Solomon agreed. Marcolfus then said, "Give me some money to pay for merchants' goods." Again Solomon agreed.

Marcolfus used the money to purchase such goods as would be valuable for a queen. When he had the goods, he and his three bands of men secretly went to the city where the pagan king was living with the queen. Marcolfus placed his men outside the city and said: "I know that if I am captured in the city I will not be able to evade death in any manner— but in that case I will ask the king that he give me permission to blow three times on my horn. When I blow the first time those dressed in black will go forward; when I blow the second blast, then those clothed in red will draw near; at the third blow, those in white will run up quickly and forcibly." Then Marcolfus entered the city with his men.

The next morning Marcolfus went to the door of the temple where the king and queen were sacrificing to their idols. He stood by and showed his wares: his head was covered by a Jewish cap. When the king and queen went forth from the temple, the queen saw some goods that were suitable for her; she asked the king to buy her a certain pretty thing, and stretched forth her hand to get it. Marcolfus struck the queen on the hand with a hazel stick, crying: "Don't you soil my goods with your bare hand!" The queen was speechless; she recognized Marcolfus, and throwing herself on the king she asked him to destroy the merchant at once, saying, "If you do not do this, we will both come to harm."

By order of the king, Marcolfus was taken and led to the court. There the king said to him: "Choose the death that you desire; you cannot live!" Marcolfus asked for a new gallows that he might hang. When this had been prepared, Marcolfus added, "Treat me as you would yourself, for I am of royal blood. According to law kings must hang on a gilded gallows." The king ordered the gallows to be gilded. When Marcolfus was brought there he asked that he might be permitted to blow his horn three times for the good of his soul. This petition was granted by the king. When Marcolfus ascended the first step he blew his first blast. Below, the group of men clothed in black came down with great noise from the hill. When the king saw the band of men he asked Marcolfus what that might be. Marcolfus said, "Devils who come for my soul." However, the queen, after she saw the men in black, hastened to the king and said; "What harm are you doing to yourself? Why don't you hang him quickly?" On the second step Marcolfus blew again, and the crowd of men dressed in red came running. The king inquired who these might be. Marcolfus said, "Hell fire comes to burn me, for I am a sinner." And when Marcolfus had blown for the third time the crowd in white sprang forward vehemently. When the king saw them, he asked who they might be, and Marcolfus said, "Miserable me, God has sent His angels for me that they might dispute over me with the devils." All this Marcolfus said to the king so that his men might have more time to gather. When the men arrived they took the king and hanged him; then they released Marcolfus, who seized the queen, cut off her nose and lips, and returned her to King Solomon.

This amazing tale was certainly known to Chrétien. In the *Cligés,* the aged doctors from Salerno seek to awaken Fenice from her feigned death, mentioning that Solomon was so detested by his wife that she deceived him by pretending to be dead (vss. 5802–5806). This is proof positive. It is, therefore, most interesting to observe how Chrétien made use of the source and adapted it for his *romanz.* In place of Marcolfus, who did not belong in his narrative, he introduced the three doctors. They make use, however, of the cruel melted lead device, just as Marcolfus did. Since Fenice was truly drugged (while Solomon's queen was not), the episode about the imitation of the bull's noise could not be used. Chrétien would probably not have used it anyhow, for this device did not suit his type of humor. Chrétien was sympathetic to young lovers. He could not let them be caught and treated cruelly.

It is possible that the bands of men dressed in black, red, and white in the Solomon story were the first suggestion for Cligés' four suits of armor—black, green, red, and white—which were worn successively at the tourney held in the field between Oxford and Wallingford (Oxford Water Meadows?) when Cligés defeated respectively Sagramor le Desreé, Lancelot, Perceval, and meets Gawain. Chrétien added one more color—green. We do not know precisely the meaning that Chrétien could have given to these colors, nor why he added the fourth. Certainly he was not following the *Solomon and Marcolfus* tale by bringing devils, hell-fire, and angels.

We *do* think, however, that Chrétien attached some symbolical significance to these colors. Cardinal Lotario di Segni, who became Pope Innocént III in 1198, proposed the color symbolism which has since persevered in the Church. Averroés (1126–98) defined the relations of colors to one another in his commentary on Aristotle. These were too late for Chrétien, we believe.[6] On the other hand, "meaningful" color may have been "in the air" among clerks when Chrétien wrote the *Cligés.* Black represented total darkness; white was complete brightness; green was a neutral color. Red was a shade below white in the spectrum; blue and violet were mitigations of black. Sagremor le Desreé, "the melancholy one," is opposed by Cligés, who is dressed in black armor; for Lancelot Cligés wears neutral green; Gawain is most superior and is opposed by Cligés clothed in "brightness"; Perceval is not yet so high on the scale of "brightness" as Gawain. Jessie L. Weston and others have argued that this Four-Day Tourney motif is similar to the Three-Day Tourney found in Huon de Rotelande's *Ipomedon,* in Ulrich von Zatzikoven's *Lanzelet,* and elsewhere. These critics have nothing special to say about the colors in Cligés' changes of armor and horses.[7]

There are four important elements in the structure of the *Cligés.* The basic theme with attendant details taken from the *Solomon and Marcolfus* at the center of the story; the Byzantine setting—this poem is the earliest of the so-called Byzantine romances; the German setting; the Arthurian setting for the courtship of Alexander and Soredamors, and for Cligés' visit to England to acquire knightly fame and prowess.

IV *Byzantine Setting*

The Byzantine setting should be taken seriously: it could have resulted from actual contact of a kind between Byzantium (and Germany) and Champagne. On the advice of St. Bernard of Clairvaux, the future count of Champagne (Henry I) waited to be knighted by Manuel Comnenos of Byzantium, in 1147. Emperor Manuel was a sworn enemy of the Norman kings of Sicily, which made him an ally of the German Emperor Conrad III, and of Frederick Barbarossa. In turn, these German rulers were in close association with Troyes and Champagne, as well as with Bar-le-Duc.[8] Stefan Hofer recalls that when Henry the Lion, duke of Saxony, invaded Magdeburg in 1170, Count Henry I of Champagne tried to reconcile Frederick Barbarossa and Louis VII of France. Many years ago (in the *Romanic Review,* XVI [1925], 43–53) we pointed out that Henry I of Troyes was threatening to remove his allegiance from the France king to the German emperor in 1160–61. We must not forget either that the mother of Henry I of Champagne was a German lady. The bringing of a young princess from Carinthia (Austria) to Troyes in 1126 to be the bride of Thibaut II, the father of Henry I, Chrétien's patron, strongly suggests the German princess who traveled far to be the bride of the Byzantine ruler in Chrétien's *Cligés.*

Byzantine influence in the story might help to explain the derivation of the name of the protagonist, Cligés. This name has a Greek appearance. Perhaps it was derived from something like Kleitias. In the great Alexander romance of the third quarter of the twelfth century there is a Clins, or Cliçon, a *compagnon* of Alexander.[9] We assume that this name is a derivative of some low-Greek name such as Kleition or Kleintios. There is a Kleitos in normal Greek, who was a milk-brother of Alexander. Chrétien might well have been familiar with some of the Alexander motifs, and could have appropriated two names from them: Alexander and Kleitias. Thessala, "the good witch" who was *mestre*, or older companion, to Fenice came from Thessaly, and that area is not very far removed from the Carinthia of Count Henry's mother. The witches of Thessaly could have been known to Chrétien from the *Metamorphoses* of Apuleius. For the name Fenice we should accept Chrétien's explanation (vss. 2725–31) that she was incomparable, like the marvelous Fenix bird.

The reason for introducing Arthur and Britain into this Byzantine material should not require explanation. Probably, after his success with *Erec and Enide,* Chrétien's head was full of the possibilities for continuing his new *Comédie Humaine*—the court of King Arthur, and the knights of the Round Table. Perhaps he was already planning to feature Lancelot, Perceval, and Gawain, as evidenced by his introducing them into the Four-Day Tourney (Sagremor did not have as much possibility). Obliged for some unknown reason to turn aside from Arthur, Chrétien elaborated the Byzantine theme of the *Solomon and Marcolfus* tale and projected this also into his new Arthurian setting.

The *Cligés* was very popular during the Middle Ages. One has only to check the references to Cligés, Fenice, and Thessala in L–F. Flutre's *Table des noms propres dans les romans du moyen-age* to be aware of this.[10] There were two adaptations of the *Cligés* in German, but fragments of only one of these have survived. In the Spanish *Cancionero de Baena*[11] there is this mention: *"Del que fiso a la Genisa Quebrantar fe e omenaje."*

The story of the *Cligés* is not a Quest. No one has ever assumed that it presented a thesis; but there is a touch in it that enables us to think of Chrétien as being something of a social reformer. The serf Jehan, the builder, is a highly skilled man who does much for his overlord Cligés. When Jehan defends before the emperor the aid given to his master, he outlines his own servile condition:

> . . . if I have done something wrong it is right for me to be taken. But I make this excuse that a serf cannot refuse anything that his proper lord commands him. One knows this to be true that I am his man—and that the wrong is his . . . I do not have anything of my own, and I do not even possess myself. Nothing belongs to me unless he grants it. (vss. 6546–58)

The base position of the serf could not be more succinctly expressed even by a modern social historian. However, Jehan was one of those sent to England to persuade Cligés and Fenice to return to take the throne of Byzantium. He must have been manumitted by that time.

CHAPTER 6

The Chevalier de la Charette,
or Lancelot

A⸀ᴛ the beginning of this poem Chrétien states:

Since my lady of Champagne wishes me to undertake a romance,
I will do so very willingly as one who is entirely at her disposal for
anything in the world that he can do; there is no flattery intended
here. Some might try this who would be wishing to flatter. Such
a person would say, and agree with this, that she is a lady who
surpasses all other living ladies, just as the *foehn* [a warm, dry Alpine
wind] is superior to other winds—the *foehn* which blows in May or
in April. Really, I am not the kind who just wants to praise his lady.
Shall I say that what a gem is worth among pearls and sardine
stones, that much is the Countess worth among queens? No, I will
say nothing about this; but this is true despite me. So much will
I say, that her desire works more in this present effort than any skill
or trouble I might put into it. Chrétien begins this book about the
Knight of the Cart. The Countess provided the meaning [*san*] and
the plot [*matière*]; [Chrétien] undertakes to think about it, adding
nothing except his trouble and intention. His narrative begins forth-
with. (vss. 1–30)

Chrétien's assertion here is very clear and has a strong note
of sincerity. He says that his lady, Countess Marie of Champagne, is a very superior person, that she has given him the

plot and meaning of his narrative, and that he himself is contributing only the trouble and time to put it all together.

Chrétien did not, however, complete the poem, for another clerk names himself later:

> The clerk Godefroi de Leigni has finished this Knight of the Cart. He should not be blamed for adding to what Chrétien has written, for he has done this with the good grace of Chrétien who began it. He has begun at the point where Lancelot was walled in, and has continued to the end. He has not wished to add anything to hurt the narrative. (vss. 7102–7112)

Indeed, Godefroi did an excellent job, though one cannot be sure of the precise line where he took over.

The combined poem was very popular. It was at the base of the great prose *Lancelot* of the thirteenth-century Vulgate cycle. (It is this prose *Lancelot* which the spirit of Francesca da Rimini mentions to Dante and his guide Vergil: "We read one day for delight about Lancelot, how love constrained him" [*Inferno*, V, vss. 127–28].) Wendelin Foerster, however, believed that the prose *Lancelot* and Chrétien's poem were based upon a common source, now lost. Many think that the Middle High German *Lanzelet* of Ulrich von Zatzikhoven, composed around 1194–95, also derived from the lost source used by Chrétien and by the author of the Vulgate compilation.[1] Imitating this prose Vulgate version were a Middle Low German rhymed version, a High German variant in prose, an account in Scottish prose of the fifteenth century, and certain sections of Malory's *Morte d'Arthur*. There is a fifteenth century German prose version by Ulrich Futerer, and another prose narrative based on Futerer. A late work in Portuguese also exists.

Many scholars believe there was a lost original for Chrétien's romance. Perhaps this is true; but we prefer to take Chrétien at his word, and postulate that Marie de Champagne was the author of the material which he rhymed. She was much concerned with Courtly Love, and doubtless Chrétien's romance conformed to her doctrine. It is possible that Marie had read another work previously which gave the substance of what she passed on to Chrétien. We doubt this; but that *could* have been the lost source.

Chrétien's *Chevalier de la Charette* is preserved for us in six manuscripts: B. N. frç. 794 (C), 12560 (T), 1450 (F), Vatican MS Christina 1724, Chantilly MS 572, and Escorial M. iii. 21. The edition prepared by Wendelin Foerster (Halle: Niemeyer, 1899) has 7,134 lines; that of Mario Roques, based on MS C, has 7,112 lines. Foerster's text was a composite one, using all manuscripts.

I *Résumé*

At the request of Marie de Champagne, Chrétien undertakes to tell the *Chevalier de la Charette*. It begins on Ascension Day after a feast at Camelot. Meleagant arrives with a challenge for Arthur: he will release captives from Arthur's kingdom whom he now holds in his land of Gorre, if Arthur will risk Guenevere, his queen, in the care of some champion who will defend her in single combat. If the champion defeats Meleagant, the prisoners will be released; if the champion loses, the queen must join them.

Having heard this, the seneschal Kay threatens to quit the court; to retain him Arthur grants him any wish. Kay desires to defend Guenevere and, though grieved, Arthur does not break his promise. Kay is defeated and afterwards, Gawain, who was nearby, sees a knight coming out of the woods in a great sweat (we learn later that this is Lancelot). The knight borrows a horse from Gawain and returns to the fray. Later Gawain again finds him on foot. Lancelot overtakes a cart driven by a dwarf and although this is a symbol of shame and degradation, after a second's hesitation he mounts therein. The dwarf promises to tell him the next day about the fate of the queen. Followed by Gawain, Lancelot is driven to a castle where he passes the night on a forbidden bed. At midnight a lance with a burning pennon barely misses Lancelot and sets the bed aflame. He extinguishes the fire, throws the lance into the middle of the room, and sleeps peacefully till morning.

At daybreak Lancelot and Gawain see the queen following a funeral procession, but are unable to overtake her. On the road they meet a girl who tells them that Guenevere has been taken to Gorre, from whence no stranger ever returns. There are two bridges which lead there: Gawain chooses the "water-bridge," which is a foot and a half wide, with water above and below; to Lancelot is left the "sword-bridge," which is as thin as a sword-blade. They separate. Lancelot rides on, absorbed in thoughts of Guenevere, and does not heed the three challenges of the guardian of the ford, who then unseats him. Startled, Lancelot defeats the guardian, but spares his life. Late in the afternoon Lancelot meets another girl, who offers him shelter in her castle if he will sleep with her that night.

Lancelot somewhat haltingly agrees, and soon they come to a castle where they feast and the girl prepares for bed. As Lancelot goes to join her he hears the girl crying for help from another room. He goes to her aid and successfully fights off seven men, then joins her in bed. She sees his reluctance and discomfort; so they sleep apart. In the morning he agrees to let her accompany him, and they ride until they near a spring beside which the girl sees a comb belonging to Guenevere. She attempts to divert Lancelot, but he will not leave the beaten path. He notices the comb and the girl laughs because he does not recognize it as Guenevere's. Hearing this he almost falls from his horse in joy; he picks the queen's golden hairs from the comb and then they proceed.

On a narrow path in a forest they meet a knight who challenges Lancelot, hoping to win the girl. They agree to seek an open spot for combat, and coming out of the woods they enter a meadow where there are many knights and ladies at play. These immediately recognize Lancelot as the disgraced knight who had ridden in a cart, and the knight's father has his son seized rather than allow him to fight such a base person. The father agrees, nevertheless, to follow Lancelot to see if he might prove of good character.

That afternoon they come to a monastery. Lancelot follows an old monk into the cemetery, where he sees tombs prepared for Gawain, Yvain, and others. He inquires about one extremely large and elaborate tomb, and learns that it is destined for whoever can lift its lid, for that knight will release the prisoners in Gorre. Lancelot easily lifts it, then refuses to reveal his identity, either to the monk or to the girl. She leaves him. As Lancelot rides on, the old knight and his son arrive, hear of his might, and wisely decide to return home.

The Chevalier de la Charette, *or* Lancelot

Pursuing his way alone, Lancelot meets with a vavassor from Logres who has been detained in Gorre with his family. Lancelot spends the night with them and is warned of his next peril, the "stony-pass" (*li passages des pierres*). He sets out in the morning accompanied by two sons of the vavassor, one a knight and the other a youth (*valet*). At the pass Lancelot is again insulted about his mounting the cart. He defeats the guardian, and the sergeants retreat without attacking.

Farther along the three meet a local man who offers them shelter for the night. As they are nearing his manor a squire approaches and tells of a revolt of the people of Logres, led by a new champion (Lancelot). The man rides ahead and escapes through his wall, trapping Lancelot and his companions between sliding gates (*portes colanz*). When a magic ring, given to Lancelot by the Lady of the Lake, will not free them, they force a postern, then ride to aid their countrymen. At evening the battle is cut short, and the people of Logres vie for the honor of lodging Lancelot.

In the morning Lancelot sets off with the sons of the vavassor again. At nightfall, while they are enjoying a meal prepared by a second kindly vavassor, another knight insults Lancelot. In the ensuing combat Lancelot emerges victorious and gives the challenger the choice of death or the indignity of himself mounting a cart. The knight refuses the cart, but begs for mercy. At this moment a maiden arrives, riding on a yellow mule, and demands the head of the defeated knight. Lancelot, torn between generosity (*largece*) and pity (*pitiez*), decides that to satisfy both he will fight the knight a second time: should he lose again, he must die. Lancelot defeats him easily and presents his head to the girl, who promises to reward him in due course. Those of the household rejoice at their guest's success, and all return to the meal.

The next evening Lancelot comes to the sword-bridge, which he crosses despite multiple cuts on his hands and feet. On the opposite shore he does not encounter the (imaginary) lions he had thought to find there, but sees instead a mighty tower from which King Bademagu and his son Meleagant have observed his difficult crossing of the sword-bridge. The virtuous king, impressed with Lancelot's bravery, insistantly counsels his villainous son to deliver over Guenevere without a fight. Meleagant refuses, even after his father promises to support Lancelot in the combat. The king goes to succor the wounded Lancelot, and offers him arms and repose before his fight with Meleagant. Lancelot wants no arms but his own and will not delay the battle past the morrow.

Before a great crowd they begin their struggle. Lancelot seems to be weakening, until he realizes that the queen herself is watching. Sparked by his love for the queen and by hatred of his adversary, Lancelot strikes with renewed vigor and would have killed Meleagant had not the King bid Guenevere stop the fight. Meleagant is incensed at this insult to his prowess, and agrees to give up the queen only if Lancelot will fight him again within a year.

King Bademagu leads Lancelot before Guenevere, but both men are dumbfounded at her refusal to thank Lancelot or, indeed, even to look at her deliverer before retiring to her room. They go to Kay, who says that Lancelot has shamed him by performing the deed at which he [Kay] had failed. Lancelot receives assurances that Guenevere has had good treatment at the hands of Bademagu, but his attempts to understand her recent snub come to naught.

Lancelot now sets off to find Gawain. The people of Gorre, thinking to please their king, seize the unarmed knight and wish to keep him prisoner. Rumors of his death at their hands arrive at court, and Bademagu is most displeased. Guenevere, on hearing these reports, retires to her room to grieve for the love she now recognizes, and wishes to follow him in death. False reports of *her* death reach Lancelot, who attempts to end his own life by hanging himself from his saddlebow (*arçon*) with his belt. When his attempt fails, he wonders which is more pitiless: the life which desires (*desirre*) him, or the death which refuses to kill him.

Lancelot reflects upon the nature of his crime toward his lady and decides that she must resent the shame of the cart. He argues to himself that one who loves truly must be prepared to undergo any travail or shame for his love, and to do whatever love bids. He is returned to the court, where he is released by Bademagu and allowed to see Guenevere, who receives him joyfully this time. He learns from her that she was angered not because he mounted the cart, but because he had *hesitated* before doing so. Lancelot arranges to be outside her window that night—they must remain separated because Kay is in her room recovering from his wounds, and the door is locked and guarded well.

Lancelot comes, but the grill is an insupportable barrier. With Guenevere's permission Lancelot silently bends the bars, but not without cutting his finger deeply. Careful not to waken Kay, he slips into the room, and lies all that night with the queen. In the morning the sheets are stained with blood from his finger. He straightens the bars and returns to his own room, genuflecting before he leaves. Meleagant arrives and sees the bloody sheets. Assuming that the sheets are bloody from Kay's wounds, he suspects that Kay slept with Guenevere during the night. Guenevere explains that she must have had a nose-bleed, but this does not keep the jealous Meleagant from telling his father, who accepts the evidence. Kay, disregarding his wounds, wishes to defend his honor, but at Guenevere's suggestion Lancelot offers to champion him. Meleagant accepts the challenge and before the combat each swears on holy relics.

As before, the fight is stopped by the mutual consent of Bademagu and Guenevere. Lancelot then sets off to find Gawain at the "water-bridge." He is led astray by a dwarf who, Lancelot's friends are convinced, was sent by Meleagant, and is confined. Meanwhile, Gawain is rescued from the "water-bridge," told about the dwarf, and taken to Bademagu, who initiates a search for Lancelot. A letter comes with Lancelot's signature, saying he is safe at Arthur's court, and asking Guenevere, Gawain, and Kay to join him there. When they reach the court they discover that the letter was a forgery.

In time, word reaches the detained Lancelot that a tournament has been arranged and that the queen is expected there. Lancelot obtains temporary release from the wife of the seneschal, his captor, by promising to return immediately after the tournament, and to give her his love. He arrives incognito and fights well until the queen requests that he do his "worst." He complies, which permits her to test his true love. The next day she tests him in like manner. Doubly assured of his love, she asks now that he do his "best." Those knights who had mocked him the previous day recognize their error, and the girls all wish to marry him. But, true to his word, Lancelot returns to Gorre in secret.

(Chrétien's account ends here.)

Meleagant hears of this incident, however, and has Lancelot sealed into a specially devised tower. He then comes to Arthur's court and challenges Lancelot to combat within a year; but agrees to accept Gawain as substitute should Lancelot not be there. He returns to Gorre and brags that Lancelot was afraid to meet him. Bademagu upbraids him for his boastful pride, and his sister, to whom Lancelot accorded the head of her enemy when she came to him on the yellow mule, resolves to discover his whereabouts, for she suspects he is imprisoned somewhere in Gorre. After more than a month's wanderings, unaccompanied, she discovers the tower. She hears Lancelot lamenting within, identifies herself, and gives him a pick with which to dig his way out. After recovering at her castle, he sets out for Arthur's court.

Meleagant has arrived at the court prepared to meet his challenge. Gawain arms himself to fight, but at this moment Lancelot arrives. In spite of Gawain's willingness to fight for him, he prefers to meet Meleagant personally. They meet in the plain before the assembled court and King Arthur himself. Lancelot cuts off the head of Meleagant after a brief battle and is led away amid great joy.

II *Poem of Ulrich von Zatzikhoven*

It is important to examine in some detail the *Lanzelet* of Ulrich von Zatzikhoven, as this was the product of a milieu close to Chrétien's. Ulrich claimed that he had adapted his work from a book brought to Germany by Hugh of Morville when he came as one of the hostages to replace Richard I in the prison at Dürnstein. Hugh was one of the murderers of St. Thomas Becket. These hostages remained in Austria from February till December of 1194. In this way we can date the *Lanzelet,* although it is true that Ulrich could have composed his own poem sometime after the hostages had left for England. This is the narrative:

Lanzelet is the son of Pant, king of Gennewis, by his wife Clarine. The people revolt and the royal family are obliged to flee. Pant dies and Lanzelet is carried to the Land of the

Maidens. He does not know his name or his family, and the fairy who raises him refuses to reveal these facts until he has defeated the best knight in the world, Iweret of Belforet. When he sets out, Lanzelet does not know how to fight; he is instructed by Johfrit de Liez.

He arrives at Galagandreiz in the company of two other knights. The daughter of the lord of this castle has been condemned to perpetual virginity by her father. She offers herself to all three of the visitors. Lanzelet kills her father and wins the girl.

He begins another series of adventures and has trouble at Limors, where he is saved by the lord's niece, whose name is Ade. He escapes from prison, fights a giant, two lions, and the lord of Limors. He becomes Ade's lover. (His wife, the girl at Galagandreiz, is not mentioned again.) Arthur sends Gawain to bring this wonderful knight to his court. Gawain and Lanzelet fight, not recognizing each other—but they stop in order to attend a tournament announced by King Lot and Gurnemanz. Lanzelet attends and fights in a Three Day tourney, with armor of a different color on each succeeding day. After victory he rides back to Ade and her brother, not having been recognized by anyone at the tourney. They reach the Castle of Death, which is held by the magician Mabuz, son of the fairy who raised Lanzelet. There is a drawbridge and everyone who passes over it loses his courage. Lanzelet is made prisoner, and at this point, Ade and her brother drop out of the story.

Iweret of Belforet, the great knight, lives near this castle and often comes there to raid. Mabuz makes Lanzelet his champion. Lanzelet rides to a fountain and strikes three times on a metal plate. Iweret's daughter, Iblis, dreams about him. Lanzelet slays Iweret, marries Iblis, and becomes the lord of Belforet. A messenger then arrives from the fairy, announcing to him his name and family. The fairy had stolen him in order to get a champion for her son Mabuz.

Lanzelet wants to find Gawain. A squire tells him that a certain King Falerin has come to Arthur's Court, claiming Guenevere. He says she had been betrothed to him before she married Arthur. Lanzelet frees her from this Falerin.

Next comes an adventure at Pluris. Lanzelet defeats a hundred knights, forgets about Iblis, and takes the lady of this castle as his fourth wife. Iblis is successful in a chastity test. Four knights go looking for Lanzelet: Gawain, Erec, Tristan, and Caheriet. They find him; his fourth wife now leaves the story. In the meantime, Falerin has carried off Guenevere and holds her in a castle surrounded by snakes. The enchanter Mabuz saves the queen, but demands that Erec and Gawain be returned to him. A giant aids Lanzelet in saving Erec and Gawain,, and all then go to Arthur's court. Iblis mentions to Lanzelet the Quest of the *Fier Baisier* ("Proud Kiss"): a dragon speaks with a human voice and demands a kiss. This quest is accomplished and the dragon becomes a woman—she had been turned into a dragon for betraying the conventions of Courtly Love. Lanzelet wins back his father's kingdom and retires to Belforet with Iblis. They have four children. They grow old, and both die on the same day.

The style of this German work is unpolished and the conglomeration of motifs resembles very much a rehash of episodes from the romances of Chrétien, as well as from *Li Beaus Desconeus* of Renaut de Beaujeu. The *Fier Baisier* is the quest that motivates the *Beaus Deconeus* or *Bel Inconnu*. Note that the kiss of a handsome knight is required to transform the lady who had been false to the rules of Courtly Love. The reader might bear in mind my suggestion in *Chrétien, Troyes, and the Grail* (1959) that the symbolism behind Chrétien's *Chevalier de la Charette* could have been that Lancelot was seeking to rescue Guenevere from some violation of the rules of Courtly Love (pp. 45–46).

It is stated in the *Lanzelet* that Lanzelet was brought up by a water fairy. In Chrétien's *Lancelot* or *Chevalier de la Charette* it is said that Lancelot had a magic ring which was given him by the fairy who had reared him. In the *Erec and Enide* (vs. 1674) his name is given in full as Lancelot del Lac. We have suggested that Chrétien took his Arthurian characters from many sources when he planned the *Erec*. We do not known where he found this hero who was reared by the Lady of the Lake, presumably a fairy. In etymologizing the name one thinks of Welsh (g)*lan* "saint". A female lake spirit is a Celtic motif (Cross, *op. cit.*, F421.1). Such a spirit could keep a mortal under water (*ibid.*, F420, 52.2). The Vulgate prose *Lancelot*, which we have mentioned earlier, developed further this lady of the lake. Lancelot's mother, Elaine, left her baby beside a neighboring lake; when she returned she saw a fairy disappear with him into the water. Lancelot grew up with this fairy and becomes a gentle, brave, young man. When he was eighteen, the fairy visited King Arthur and asked him to give knighthood to Lancelot on St. John's day. So far as we know, this account of Lancelot and the fairy was put together in the post-Chrétien period. But Chrétien definitely had some idea of Lancelot's being the ward of a fairy.

III *Sources*

Having presented these summaries, we pass to an outline of what most Arthurian scholars believe to be the background of this romance by Chrétien. One of the two main motifs is the abduction of Guenevere by Meleagant, which many, chiefly W. A. Nitze and Tom Peete Cross,[2] have identified with the abduction of the fairy Winlogee, portrayed, they say, on the tympanum of the Arthurian Portal at the Cathedral of Modena. Meleagant would be Melvas, or Maheloas of Somersetshire, an Otherworld chief associated with Glastonbury. According to the Latin *Vita Gildae* (1150), written by Caradoc of Llancarvan, which contains much Celtic mythology, this Melwas carried Guenevere to Glastonbury (*Urbs Vitrea*), the abbot of Glastonbury and King Arthur forced him to give her up. The *Vita Gildae* rendered the name Glastonbury by Inis Gutri ("Island of Glass"), which has been associated by some with the Celtic Otherworld. (Gastonbury is not actually an island; in early times it was completely surrounded by marshes.) In the manuscript R text of the *Erec et Enide,* transcribed by Foerster, it is recorded that Melvas of Isle Voirre attended the wedding of Erec and Enide. But manuscript B. N. 794, which is used by Mario Roques as the basis for his edition, changes the name of the individual to Moloas and he is said to be lord of the Isle Noire. We quote the passage in question from *Erec et Enide* (vss. 1895–1901):

Along with those whom I have named came Moloas, a rich baron, lord of the Black Isle. No one has ever heard it thunder there, nor do there fall thunder and tempest. No toad or serpent stays there, nor is it warm or wintry . . .

Although we do not agree with those who believe that Chrétien wrote his *Chevalier de la Charette* primarily to exploit this Celtic abduction theme, we are ready to agree that this Celtic tale was known to our poet, and that he adapted it in his romance.

It is quite clear that Courtly Love is the principal theme in the Lancelot.[3] In order to win his lady, to show that he is completely subservient to her, Lancelot "shames" himself on various occasions. The most notable occasion, which gave Chrétien the title for this poem, occurs when Lancelot climbs into a cart behind a scurrilous dwarf. Apropos of this, Lancelot later says: "Whatever one does for his lady is love and courtesy . . ." (vss. 4377–78), "When it seems to be an honor to do what Love desires, even to climb into a Cart, she should consider this as love, and proof positive that Love tests his own and thereby knows who they are" (vss. 4387–93). When Guenevere is cool to Lancelot (vss. 3975–87) she gives as her reason: "What? Were you not ashamed to enter the Cart when you hesitated? Very unwilling were you to climb into it when you hesitated for two steps. That is why I did not wish to talk to you or look at you" (Vss. 4502–7). The details of his entering the cart were known, mysteriously, by a wide circle of those whom Lancelot met later. In each of his subsequent "trials" he is sneered at because of this, and the queen is so well informed of the minutest details of the adventure that she even knows he had a slight hesitation. (Gawain, who was with him, would not climb in at all, although invited to do so by the dwarf.)

The other great test, in true Courtly Love style, is when the queen sends a message to Lancelot early in the Three-Day Tourney, that he is to behave "as badly as possible." He does this on two successive days. (vss. 5658 ff.) There can be little doubt that this Courtly Love theme was proposed to Chrétien by Marie, the daughter of Eleanor of Aquitaine. It is not clear how far Courtly Love monopolizes the story, and where other motifs enter in.

The cart itself is important. Chrétien explains that a cart was considered an emblem of disgrace, since malefactors were placed in carts (vss. 323 ff.). Most modern critics have rejected this as the true meaning of cart and dwarf. Pauphilet proposed that such a cart was a symbol of Death—the Cart of Ankhou, which occurs in Breton folklore. The present writer does not feel that Jean Frappier, or anyone else, has fully established that this cart was a Celtic device.[4] In the absence of a better explanation, we are disposed to accept Chrétien's assertion that a cart was a forbidden vehicle for a knight. A dwarf was commonly considered a deformed person, a distortion of nature, and as such was usually associated with evil (Cross, G 303.2.2.3).[5] We no longer insist upon our interpretation of Gorre as a term applied to a "land of luxuriousness, of lack of moderation," although the word is discussed by Meyer-Lübke in his *Etymologisches Wörterbuch der romanischen Sprachen* (Heidelberg: Winter, 1935), no. 3821, and *did* have valid existence. If this explanation of Gorre were accepted, the courtly lover, Lancelot, would be rescuing his perfect lady, Guenevere, from a revolt against the rules of Courtly Love. (Compare the sin of the lady in the *Fier Baisier* episode of the *Lanzelet*). If we admit that Marie de Champagne's fable had to with Love subservience, it is hardly necessary to continue with further subjective analysis.

IV   *Celtic Themes*

In this romance Chrétien also made use of current motifs of Celtic origin. The abduction motif—an Irish *aided*—may well be a reflection of the Melwas-Guenevere episode, mentioned above. Chrétien could easily have been familiar with this tale where Guenevere is abducted by Melwas, which he could have obtained from the *Vita Gildae* of Caradoc, perhaps at Glastonbury Abbey itself. The kingdom of Melwas could be the Celtic Otherworld. In order to reach there, Lancelot goes through a series of trials. The land is described by the maiden whom Lancelot and Gawain encounter at the crossroad: "A knight big and large of body, son of the king of Gorre, has taken return" (vss. 641–45). Note, it is not stated that no inhabitant of the land can leave it; it is said that no *estranges*—no visitor—can get away. The name of the father of Meleaganz is Bademagus, and it is true that *magus* was a term designating a Celtic druid (Thompson, motif P 427). Certainly the barriers to be crossed before approaching into Gorre are present in Celtic folk motifs: especially the sword-bridge (Thompson, F 152.1.6) guarded by imaginary beasts (F 150.2.1). There is no specific folklore designation for an underwater bridge, but Tom Peete Cross seems to accept this concept as related to similar types of Otherworld bridges.

Aside from the shame of the cart, the kingdom of Gorre with its terrible approaches, and the characters Meleagant and Bademagu, there are other details which we must explain and identify. The castle with the flaming lance may have been another test of bravery (see Cross, H 1250.1). The trial involving the young woman who allows Lancelot to spend the night in her castle, thus testing his devotion to his lady, is clearly understandable. But what is the meaning of the scene in the graveyard where Lancelot recognizes his own tomb and alone can lift the stone that covers it? The exiles from Logres among whom Lancelot finds himself were mentioned by Meleaganz when he visited Arthur's court. Certainly they are *estranges* who could not return from Gorre, whatever this may mean. (As a matter of fact, they even failed to get across the bridges into Gorre proper.)

For some psychological factors we do not necessarily need to find folk sources. Lancelot has special charm for women. He was raised by the fairy (Lady of the Lake?) who gave him a magic ring. When he wished to take part in the Three-Day Tourney he was allowed to do so by the wife of the seneschal, his captor. When he was imprisoned on the island he was freed by the sister of Meleagant. When he was about to be deceived by a treacherous knight, before he crossed the sword-bridge, this lady came to him on a yellow mule, saying that the man was a treacherous fellow and begging for the head. When she left she promised to give Lancelot a recompense at some future date. I cannot explain these feminine "helpers" except to suggest that they have to do with Lancelot's character as a Courtly Love figure.

Two additional themes might be explained subjectively. The first is the vision Lancelot has from the upper window of the castle of the fiery lance, in which he sees the queen riding along beside Kay on a bier, with Meleaganz leading a crowd, and three damsels grieving over the figure on the bier. It might be significant that this is shortly after Lancelot has heard Mass, and that he is talking with the lady of the castle when he sees the scene.

The Chevalier de la Charette, *or* Lancelot

What are we to think of the mutual fear that the other is dead, shared by Guenevere and Lancelot before they are reconciled in Gorre? Moreover, what of the scene in Guenevere's room, in which Lancelot is "solaced" by the queen? The accusation against Kay because of the blood on the sheet may be reminiscent of the *Tristan.* As he leaves, Lancelot genuflects before the room—just as he would before an altar (vss. 4734–36). In the twelfth century a genuflection was commonly a way of acknowledging a great gift from someone; but Chrétien makes specific reference to genuflection before an altar. It is probable that the exaltation of the Lady to a higher plane, which was to culminate in the *dolce stil nuovo* doctrine of the thirteenth century, is beginning to be formulated here.

To sum up, we infer that Marie of Champagne had a Courtly Love fable in mind which she proposed to Chrétien for his elaboration. Perhaps her fable already contained some of the Celtic and other motifs which we have just outlined; on the other hand, it could be that Chrétien introduced these. He claims, however, that he added nothing "except his trouble and the *antancion,*" or basic meaning (vss. 28–30). We believe that at this time he had his *Yvain* in actual preparation, and as a result was pleased to turn over the completion of the *Knight of the Cart* to Godefroi de Leigny (vss. 7124–32). Although the *Lanzelet* in German is a composite tale made up from various themes in Chrétien, it is just possible that Ulrich von Zatzikhoven had heard a version of the same tale which Marie de Champagne gave Chrétien for elaboration.[6]

CHAPTER 7

The Yvain, *or* Chevalier au lion

T HIS romance has 6,808 lines (in the Mario Roques edition based on MS B. N. frç. 794, copied by Guiot; the edition of Wendelin Foerster, a composite text, has 6,818 lines) and is found complete in seven manuscripts: B. N. frç. 794, 1433, 1450, 12560, 12603, Vatican Christina 1725, and Chantilly 432. There are also the Montpellier fragments and those of Annonay.

Yvain is today the most popular of Chrétien's poems. When a class in Old French reads a Chrétien romance, either entire or at some length, it is almost always this one. This preference may be due to habit and academic tradition, but there is perhaps another reason. The *Yvain* narrative builds up and reaches its resolution in a way that is exciting to twentieth-century readers. The conflict between Kay and Yvain, the Generous Host, the Giant Herdsman, the Wooing of Laudine (with its piquant conversation), the ingenuousness of the girls who come upon the mad Yvain, the Lion episodes, the "sweat shop" in the castle— these are all rapidly-paced episodes which have considerable appeal for the modern reader.

But a better way to judge a medieval work is to appreciate how it reflects the conditions and tastes of its time. The *Yvain* excels in this also. Chrétien admits to considerable originality in the composition of this poem. He says at the close: "In

this way does Chrétien finish his romance of the Knight of
the Lion; he has never heard anything more about it, nor will
you ever hear anything else, unless some one wishes to falsify
it" (vss. 6804–8, ed. Marie Roques).

Note that Chrétien's own name for this poem was *Chevalier
au lyon* (vs. 6804), which must indicate the section of the
story which he wished to emphasize most—for his patron. In
the *Yvain* there are three direct references to the *Lancelot* or
Chevalier de la Charette. The first is

. . . they told me that a knight had taken away the Queen, in
which the King acted like a madman when he sent her to him
. . . and Kay, I believe, conducted her to the knight who led her
away. My lord Gawain who seeks her is now in great difficulty.
(vss. 3700–709)

The second is:

A knight from a strange land is taking away the king's wife; he
came to get her at the Court. But he could not have taken her by
any means if Kay had not deceived the King, so that he turned her
over to him [Kay] and made him her guard. Any man or woman
would be silly who would trust to *his* care . . . He [Gawain] has
gone after this fellow [Meleaganz]. (vss. 3912–33)

The third is:

And the Queen had returned only three days before from the
prison where Meleaganz had kept her. The other prisoners, and
Lancelot because of treason had stayed behind in that tower. . . .
(vss. 473–39)

This third passage has reference to the last episodes before
the Three-Day Tourney; so that Chrétien may be inferred to
have been at work on the *Lancelot* and the *Yvain* simultaneously.
In this remark, two thirds of the way before the end of the
Yvain, he mentions an episode which was nearly at the close
of his own portion of the *Lancelot.* The pattern of the title
Chevalier au lyon is to be associated with that of *Chevalier
de la Charette. Charette* is here contrasted with *Lion.*

Eugene Vinaver once made a comment apropos of the thirteenth century Vulgate Cycle which can apply as well to Chrétien:

If the Arthurian Cycle has so often been mistaken for a collection of tales haphazardly put together, it is because its mechanism is hidden behind the extraordinary complexities of the text . . . The fascination of tracing a theme through all its phases, of waiting for its return while following other themes, of experiencing the constant sense of their simultaneous presence, depends upon our grasp of the entire structure—the most elusive that has ever been devised.[1]

I Dating

Several suggestions have been made for dating the *Yvain*, but only one has definite value. In verse 595, Kay remarks grimly:

After dinner every one goes to kill Nûr-ed-Din without stirring from his seat, and now you will go to avenge Forré! Are your saddlebags packed, are your mailed *chauces* [leg coverings] rubbed up, and your banners unfurled?

Nûr-ed-Din was the sultan of Aleppo from 1146 to 1173 (1174) and was therefore the principal Saracen enemy to all those disembarking at Acre on their way to the Holy Land. It may be argued that people in France might not have known of the Sultan's death till some time . . . . , but a delay in news of this sort would not have been greater than a few months.

It is very reasonable to assume that the *Yvain* was composed before 1174. The date 1169 has been suggested. G. F. Benecke and E. Kölbing were the first to attempt proof of this earlier dating.[2] They made use of a passage in Hartmann von Aue's German version, which follows Chrétien's original very closely. Calogrenanz tells the tale of his adventure at the fountain. King Arthur then announces that he will undertake this adventure, "that he would go see the Fountain before a fortnight passes . . . so that he would arrive there on the Eve of St. John the Baptist's Day." Since Arthur was speaking on Pentecost, a movable feast, and St. John's Eve is a fixed feast, correlation between the two dates is entirely possible. The Vigil of St. John the Baptist is always June 23. Two weeks before this would set Pentecost on June 8, and that would place Easter on April 20.

This very late date for Easter is quite remarkable,but possible. If it can be assumed that Chrétien had the current "remarkable" year in mind it might be concluded that the year in question was one of these: 1147, 1158, 1169, or 1180. Of these years 1169 seems to be the best choice. The amusing thing is that the present writer, in 1922, repeated this same calculation, without any knowledge whatsoever of Benecke and Kölbing. This was read as a paper in Mario Roques' seminar in Paris and was subsequently printed in the *Romanic Review*.[3] Someone present should have been aware of the duplication. The reliability of this argument depends upon whether one can be sure that Chrétien had the current year in mind. This cannot be taken for granted; but the assumption is an interesting one.

We now give a fairly detailed summary of the plot of the *Yvain.*

II *Résumé*

The court of King Arthur is assembled at Carduel, or Carlisle, for the feast of Pentecost. After the meal the king, quite contrary to his habit, retires to his chamber with the queen, who detains him until he falls asleep. Outside the door, Kay, Gawain, and Yvain are listening to Calogrenant tell of an adventure which befell him. The queen, overhearing the tale, comes out to sit among them, and Calogrenant, vexed by an insult from Kay, continues his story only at the queen's insistence.

Seven years earlier, he says, while coming out of the wood of Broceliande, he came upon a manor house in which he was given lodging for the night by a vavassor and his daughter. In the morning, pursuing his trail, Calogrenant met a giant herdsman who told him of a marvelous rock beside a magic spring. By pouring water upon this rock from a golden basin attached to a giant evergreen tree, he caused a fearful tempest, which God quickly quieted. He was thereupon challenged and defeated by the Knight of the Fountain, managing to escape only with his life. Although he returned to the manor on foot, he was as well received as before, for he was the first who had ever so escaped.

Yvain, upon hearing this tale, expresses a great desire to pursue the adventure himself. Kay derides him. Nevertheless, he sets out, contrary to the purpose of Arthur, who intends to go there within a fortnight accompanied by his court. At the fountain, impetuous Yvian raises the storm, meets the knight (Escalados le Ros), whom he routs and pursues to his town. Passing over the drawbridge to the gate tower Yvain's horse trips a metal door which descends precipitously and severs the horse in two, narrowly missing Yvain, who finds himself in a rich entrance room within the gate. He is greeted by a girl who, in return for the kindness which he had once shown her at Arthur's court, offers him food and a magic ring which, when worn with the stone toward the palm, makes the bearer invisible. This girl, Lunette, is the *mestre* or confidante, of the lady Laudine. She disappears just as knights enter for Yvain, seeking to avenge their dead master. Yvain, however, has put on the ring, and observes their search in safety. As he is watching their efforts the funeral procession bearing Esclados passes through, and the searchers redouble their efforts when they see the corpse bleeding anew. They are urged on by the grieving widow, Laudine de Landuc, whose singular beauty enslaves Yvain. After the procession has passed outside the gate, he urges Lunette to show him some aperture from which he might observe the beautiful lady. The funeral terminated, Yvain sees Laudine remain behind alone, and he reflects upon his own condition. He realizes that the lady has captured him by love, and has thereby avenged her lord, who could not defeat him by arms.

Lunette, seeing how troubled he is, offers to help him get what he wants. She goes to Laudine and upbraids her for her excessive grief, reminding her that she must now find someone to protect her land and fountain from Arthur, who will be there within a week. Lunette argues that the worthier knight is he who wins the combat, and that a lady does no wrong in loving such a one. (Laudine is at first incensed by the idea of marrying her husband's slayer, but a night of reflection convinces her she would do no wrong thereby.) Lunette reminds her also that no knight in her court would be brave enough to take the fountain duty upon himself, and that each would willingly let it fall upon a new champion. The lady inquires about the victor, and learns he is Yvain, the son of King Urien, whereupon she commands that he appear before her the following night. The maiden, pretending to have him brought from Arthur's court, secretly bathes and outfits him in her chamber. She tells him that their ruse has been uncovered and that he is Laudine's "prisoner," but that her lady has promised to treat him with courtesy. Upon entering the lady's presence, Yvain declares his eternal love of her. This love makes him a prisoner to her every whim, and he glady agrees to undertake the defense of her fountain. Laudine is surprised and pleased by the ardor of her new suitor. She presents him to her assembled court which, to a man, approves her choice; they are wed that very day.

Arthur arrives with his suite, among them Kay, who remarks upon the absence of Yvain, suggesting that he dared not come after having foolishly boasted that he could slay the Knight of the Fountain. After Arthur pours water upon the stone, and the phenomenon is repeated, Kay asks and is granted permission to fight the Knight, who appears as expected. Yvain (for it is he) recognizes his detractor and is glad to put Kay to shame. After his victory Yvain reveals his identity and welcomes Arthur and his court to visit his new castle for a week.

Following the week's pleasure, as they are planning to leave, Gawain urges Yvain to accompany him to the tourneys, so that through deeds he may continually merit his lady's love. Yvain begs Laudine's leave, and this is granted, on condition that he return within a year at St. John's. On parting, Laudine gives him a ring which protects from all physical ills the one who wears it in true love. That year the two companions win great honors, and the term slips by unnoticed. A maiden arrives at Arthur's court at Chester and demands that Yvain return the ring since he has not proved himself a true lover—such a one would not steal the love of his lady by deceit, but would rather treasure and return it.

Yvain, insane with grief, tears his clothes and runs naked into the forest, where he lives from the meat of animals he kills and bread and drink provided by a hermit. A long time later he is found asleep by two maidens and their mistress. They recognize Yvain from the scars on his face, and hope to revive him so that he may defend their town against Count Alier. The lady gives one girl an ointment to treat his madness, and cautions her to use but a little upon his forehead (the ointment had been a gift from the fairy Morgue). The girl zealously over-anoints him, however, and to hide her shame she throws the box into a stream. Yvain recovers his senses and puts on a robe the girl has left beside him. After Yvain has clothed himself, the girl feigns to stumble upon him accidentally and conducts him to her mistress at Norison. He recovers his strength and leads the lady's knights. They repulse the attack of Count Alier. The lady wishes to reward him by marriage or with money, but Yvain accepts only her gratitude and sets forth again.

In a deep wood he sees a fire-spitting serpent holding a lion by the tail. Yvain kills the poisonous serpent and earns the esteem and gratitude of the lion, which accompanies him on his way, providing him with food and guarding his sleep at night. After a week's wandering they come upon the spring at Broceliande, where Yvain laments aloud his plight and thinks to kill himself. He is overheard by Lunette, who has been imprisoned on the seneschal's accusation that she had betrayed Laudine's trust by inducing her to love Yvain. She will only be released if she can find a knight who will champion her against three others at noon the next day. Yvain promises to return to fight for her if she will not reveal his identity. Seeking repose for the night he enters a town, which he finds threatened by the giant Harpin de la Montaingne, who will kill the four sons of the local lord unless he delivers his beautiful daughter over to be ravaged by the giant's household. Yvain offers his aid when he learns that the lord's wife is Gawain's sister. With the aid of his lion. Yvain kills the giant; he asks to be remembered only as the *chevalier au lion*. He releases the four sons, who had been shamed and scourged by a dwarf, and sets out to rescue Lunette. Yvain accepts the challenge of the seneschal and his two brothers, and promises to fight without his lion. But seeing Yvain in great need, the lion comes to his aid. The two, although both sorely wounded, carry the field, and the three false witnesses are burned on the pyre prepared for Lunette. Yvain, revealing himself only as the *chevalier au lion*, refuses Laudine's solicitude, saying he cannot tarry until he is sure of having regained his lady's favor. Leaving Laudine troubled by these strange words, he departs with his lion, and they arrive at a castle where they rest until both are healed.

Meanwhile, the lord of Noire Espine has died, leaving his inheritance to his two daughters. The elder wishes to claim it all, and goes to Arthur's court where she induces Gawain to champion her. The younger sister, with forty days to find a champion, sets out in search of the famed *chevalier au lion*. She falls ill from fatigue, but the pursuit is continued by a friend who, after passing by the dead bodies of Harpin and Lunette's accusers, finally overtakes Yvain. She apologizes for the other's absence, and convinces Yvain to support the younger sister's rightful claims.

Riding on, they arrive at the town of Pesme Aventure, where they wish to pass the night. The townspeople warn them that to enter the castle would be to their woe. With nowhere else to lodge, however, they resolve to stop there. Upon entering the castle yard they see three hundred maidens, wan and poorly clad, sewing and weaving beautiful cloths. One informs them that the king of the Isle of Maidens sends thirty girls there each year as perpetual ransom to two sons that a devil had engendered and who had spared his life in his youth. They will only be delivered when some knight defeats the two half-devils. Yvain, after a good night of feasting and resting provided by the lord and his daughter, challenges and defeats the two with the aid of his lion. The lord wishes to reward Yvain with his daughter and his wealth, but he refuses and asks only the release of the three hundred, which is granted.

Yvain continues on his way, meets the girl he is to champion, and they arrive on the fortieth day at Arthur's court. The eldest sister will accept no compromise, so Gawain and Yvain meet that day in mortal combat. Neither recognizes the other, and each is driven on by the hate that coexists with love in his heart. They fight fiercely and evenly till night falls, when they retire, each with full respect for the other's might. They reveal their names, and in astonishment, and in horror and love for one other, each claims to have been defeated. Arthur intervenes and awards the younger sister her claim, but insists that she acknowledge her fealty to her sister. At this moment the lion comes seeking his master, and Gawain realizes that the celebrated *chevalier au lion* who had succored his niece and nephews is Yvain.

But Yvain cannot be happy until he regains Laudine's favor, so he sets out in secret toward the fountain, and again causes the terrible storm. Lunette reminds her mistress that they have no defender, but that they might have one if the *chevalier au lion* who slew the giant and the three knights could be reconciled with his lady. Laudine swears to do all in her power to effect such a reconciliation. Lunette, overjoyed, sets out to find Yvain, and is surprised to see that he is the one at the fountain. She tells him of her lady's pledge, and leads him fully armed before her. Laudine receives him graciously, but is shocked to discover that he is none other than her husband Yvain. Thus tricked, she keeps her promise rather than be guilty of perjury. The two are peacefully reconciled; Yvain recognizes his folly and pledges henceforth to be constant.

III   *Sources of Names and Episodes*

A tremendous amount has been written on the meaning of the episodes in this romance. It is not possible to examine all these suggestions here, but we can generalize on some of them.

That Yvain was the son of Urien was drawn by Chrétien from Wace's *Brut*, where Arthur assigns the kingdom of Lothian to his brother-in-law Lot; Scotland to Lot's brother Anguselus; and Moray (or Rheged) to their brother Urien, or Urian.[4] These names, and their appointments by Arthur, came originally from Geoffrey of Monmouth's *History of the Kings of Britain*.[5] Edmond Faral defines Lothian as the name of the region immediately south of the Firth of Forth; Scotland proper, he says, was the district just north of the Forth—and Moray probably combined what is now Moray, Nairn, and Banff. It is rather obvious to a Celticist that Yvain is derived from Owein (from Eugenios, or possibly from early British *Esu-genos* "well born"). Faral insists that Lot, Anguselus, and Urien were names invented by Geoffrey.[6] Urien could not be in this category because it represents early British *Urbi-genos*.[7] Sixth-century history is imperfectly known as there are no reliable chronicles from that period. But there is evidence in early Welsh poetry that the bard Taliesin may have been household poet to Urien and his son Owein. There are twelve poems which can reasonably be assigned to Taliesin. Urien and Owein almost certainly were prominent chieftains in the last half of the sixth century.[8]

The *Yvain* or *Chevalier au Lion* has two obvious divisions: the episode of the Magic Fountain and the episode of the Lion. As Mrs. Sargent and others have inferred, these two divisions were not placed together haphazardly; they represent a logical development in plot and in the character of the protagonist. But we must not assume that 'Chrétien found them together in a common source. As is always true in the study of medieval literature, the critic must not confuse the purpose, or symbolism, followed by the poet, with the source elements which chanced to be used. The distinction between *matière* and *sens* must be maintained.

There are numerous elements in the *Yvain* which we should like to trace: the Generous Host and his beautiful daughter who live at the "entrance to the adventure"; the giant herdsman who informs the knights about the Fountain; the episode of the Magic Fountain and the marriage to the slain husband's widow. In the second part there are the Grateful Lion, the ointment given by the Fairy Morgue, the rescue from the evil Giant, the adventure of Pesme Aventure, the "sweat shop," the other characters mentioned, such as the king of the Isle of Maidens, and the *Netuns* or half-devils. It is not difficult to assume that these episodes were drawn from folklore; but we should like to be more precise than this. Some scholars assume that Chrétien had heard a more primitive Celtic tale about the Magic Fountain—and that this could be a lost original which was used also by the Welsh storyteller who wrote down the *Lady of the Fountain* (or, as it can be called, *Owein and Lunete*). It is rather generally agreed that the primary source for the Grateful Lion was some variant of the Greek Androcles and the Lion story (first narrated, in ancient times, by Aulus Gellius, who wrote his *Attic Nights* in Athens). We know that the concept of an *Insula Puellarum,* "Land of the Maidens" (*Tir nan-Ingen*), is present in the Celtic voyage texts.

IV   *The Magic Fountain*

Marvelous fountains are occasionally listed in rather sober medieval writings, notably among the Celts. In his *Itinerary through Wales* Giraldus Cambrensis mentions several such lakes:

The lake of Brecheinoc is celebrated for its miracles; for, as we have before observed, it sometimes assumes a greenish hue, so in our days it has appeared to be tinged with red . . . Moreover it is sometimes seen by the inhabitants covered and adorned with buildings, pastures, gardens, and orchards. In the winter when it is frozen over, and the surface of the water is converted into a shell of ice, it emits a horrible sound resembling the moans of many animals collected together . . .[9]

Giraldus in the same treatise speaks of "two lakes worthy of admiration" on top of Mount Snowdon. Chrétien's Magic Fountain was undoubtedly the Fountain of Berenton in the Forest of Broceliande in Brittany. As the action of the *Yvain* begins in Carlisle in northwest England (Logres), and there is no hint of any crossing of the Channel, we can suppose that Chrétien introduced this Breton fountain into his romance without any thought of geography. He had heard of this miraculous fountain from some source, and it suited the development of his story.

The sober-minded chronicler Wace heard the same legend about this fountain and made a special journey to investigate it. We translate from his *Rou*:

. . . Broceliant is a forest very long and wide in Brittany about which the Bretons tell fables—it is much celebrated. In one part of it the Fountain of Berenton springs out beside a rock. Hunters used to go there frequently in the great heat to draw the water for their bodies and to pour it on the rock. In this way they would have rain—it would rain in the forest and all around. I do not know why. They are used to seeing fairies there, if the Bretons are being truthful, and many other strange things. There used to be eyries of hawks there and a great quantity of large stags; but the farmers have cleared these out. I went there to find marvels. I saw the forest and I saw the land. I looked for wonderful things but I did not find them; I was a fool to go there and I came away like a fool. I looked for foolishness and I considered myself silly. (vss. 6395–6420)[10]

Bishop Jacques de Vitry (who had great interest in folk legends) wrote: "In Lesser Britain there is said to be a certain fountain of which the water when poured on a nearby stone is believed to provoke rain and thunder."[11] There can be no doubt whatsoever that Chrétien had heard mention of this particular fountain in Broceliande. But we still do not know why he chose to introduce it into his *Yvain*.

V *Meaning of the* Yvain

It is also important to determine whether Chrétien brought together his source materials only with the idea of telling a good story (allowing, of course, for the fact that he added to his sources his charm and his skill as a psychologist and as an observer of manners and customs), or whether he had some spiritual or diactic theme which he hoped to express in a symbolic way. In a recent doctoral dissertation, J. H. Reason has answered this clearly: "The fact that Chrestien was a man of the twelfth century is sufficient proof that he wished to teach a lesson, that he purported to do more than entertain his readers by a pattern of narration. . . ."[12]

Julian Harris believes that the second part of the *Yvain* depicts the spiritual and moral rehabilitation of the protagonist. A chapel is mentioned. Laudine could be reconciled either through paganism or through Christian ideals. Perhaps the entire *Yvain* narration is an account of expiation. The knight Calogrenanz sees a phenomenon which he is not worthy of solving; Yvain succeeds at first, then fails through lack of Grace of some kind. He acquires this while in the company of the grateful Lion. The importance of the Lion is suggested by the fact that Chrétien mentioned the beast in the title for his entire narrative.[13]

Süheyla Bayrav also sees in the Lion episode a kind of purification for transgression against love in the first part of the romance: Bayrav admits that what Chrétien meant to say can be comprehended only in the light of Christianity.[14]

Yvain, who had won control of the magic fountain, failed greatly in his love when he failed to return in time to his wife. Since he was brave and generous, a Grace for that occasion, in the form of a lion, helped him to climb again the calvary of Penitence. His constancy, his humility, his charity restored to him finally the love of his lady.

In his *De Naturis Rerum,* Alexander Neckam makes a clear ethical allusion to a fountain (although it is not certain that he has the passage from Chrétien in mind):

Concerning a spring whose water, when drawn up and cast upon a stone, causes a tempest to arise. They claim that [there is such a spring] . . . It is true that much rain suddenly comes about, with hail and vehement wind. Who dares determine where this storm comes from? The stone signifies the inflexible mind from which, if you do not wish to cool off or soften it by the waters of the doctrine of Holy Scripture, suddenly and tumultuous disdain will arise.[15]

Apparently Vincent of Beauvais (in his *Speculum Naturale,* Bk. VI) repeated this description from Alexander without the symbolism. But Huon de Mery, in his *Tournoiement de l'Antichrist* (early thirteenth century) had Chrétien in mind when he said that a knight of Saint-Louis went to visit this marvelous spring, and while seeing it exclaimed that, "In clearer Christian water one never received baptism." Then Huon describes the marvelous singing of the birds and remarks that this is the opening of the heavens to reveal God in all his glory.[16]

Bringing together these details and others, Maxwell S. Luria treats the episode of the Magic Spring as a "symbolic baptism followed by a beatific vision of salvation." He interprets the whole *Yvain* as a narrative of a protagonist who undergoes the trial of the fountain, achieves moral regeneration, and then (after backsliding) once more recovers, through purgative adventures "which constitute the body of the romance," and finally becomes reconciled to Laudine and to the true meaning of Love. Esclados represents the demonic principle. The storm of the fountain is a divine initiation.[17]

We are in sympathy with the general principle of such interpretations, although we must admit that such detailed conclusions can have no certainty.

Auerbach commented eloquently that the feudal romance, as represented in Chrétien, has for its fundamental principle the portrayal of knighthood's mores and ideals. The *vavassor* at whose dwelling Calogrenanz and Yvain first call has a knightly duty to offer hospitality. It is strange that he gives no warning of what is to follow at the Spring, or Fountain. His knightly reticence is to be contrasted with the free talk of the strange peasant who herds the bulls. The adventures of Calogrenant and Yvain, Auerbach says, are "a fated and graduated test of election"—only Yvain "proves capable of sustaining the adventure."[18]

The manor house on the edge of the forest which is occupied by the agreeable vavassor and his daughter has nothing strange in its appearance except the sheet of copper which hangs on a post in the courtyard. The host strikes this three times with a hammer in order to summon his people. Pauphilet has suggested that this manor and its inhabitants could signify the entrance into the Land of the Dead.[19]

Jean Frappier believes that the first part of the Yvain is based upon a *conte d'aventure* of a primitive type—the same one which served also as a source for the Welsh *Owein and Lunete,* to which we have referred. This contained the Fountain, the Generous Host, and the Herdsman. Laudine was the fairy of the Fountain, and Lunette was another fairy. In the Castle of the *Pesme Aventure* ("Evil Adventure"), Yvain slays the two half-devils and rescues the three hundred maidens—this is another survival of the Celtic Otherworld. Frappier agrees that the Lion theme is derived from Androcles and the Lion. To these folklore sources, Frappier says, Chrétien has added some clever scenes of his own—notably the scenes between Laudine and Lunete, which he designates as a *fabliau*. Chrétien, he says, has real dramatic qualities in his dialogue. There is also a lyric accent found in regrets for the olden days, and in melancholy departures. Frappier insists that Chrétien was concerned first of all with the literary beauty of this work; but he wished also to show what course was wise in the conflict between Love and Chivalry. The eventual attainment of happiness could come only after a long series of misadventures and personal trials. Frappier adds that there are numerous details taken from contemporary life and, of course, that there are parallels drawn from Ovid and from other Old French romances of the time, especially the *Eneas* and the *Thebes*.[20] Jean Frappier's estimate is good, and is not imbued with the exaggeration typical of so many of the *Celtisants*. However, we prefer the idea of some Christian symbolism.

Foerster, of course, was convinced of the Androcles and the Lion source. He insisted also that the theme of the easily consoled widow had its origins in the Jocasta-Oedipus story. There is also, he says, the possibility of the Widow of Ephesus motif. Foerster believes that the *Lanzelet* of Ulrich von Zatzikoven has episodes which parallel the earlier part of the *Yvain*, and he argues that these go back to a common source. There is folklore material here, Foerster admits, but he does not believe it was Celtic.

VI *Other Suggestions*

During the past seventy-five years many scholars have taken somewhat extreme positions in explaining the sources of the *Yvain:* These include, R. S. Loomis, in his *Celtic Myth and Arthurian Romance* (New York: Columbia University Press, 1927); Lucy A. Paton, in her *Studies in the Fairy Mythology of Arthurian Romance* (reprint, New York: Burt Franklin, 1960); W. A. Nitze, in his "A New Source of the Yvain," *Modern Philology*, III (1905), 278–79; A. C. L. Brown in his *Iwain: A Study in the Origin of Arthurian Romance* (Cambridge, Mass.: Harvard Studies and Notes in Philology and Literature, VIII, 1903); Oliver M. Johnston, in his "The Episode of Yvain, the Lion, and the Serpent in Chrétien de Troyes," *Zeitschrift für französische Sprache und Literatur*, XXI (1907); W. A. Nitze, in his "The Fountain Defended," *Modern Philology*, VII (1909), 151–53; A. C. L. Brown, in his "Chrétien's *Yvain*," *Modern Philology*, IX (1911–12), 109–28; and C. B. Lewis, in his *Classical Mythology and Arthurian Romances, A Study of the Sources of Chrestien de Troyes' Yvain and Other Arthurian Romances* (New York: Oxford University Press, 1932). Also of considerable interest are G. L. Hamilton, "Storm-Making: Rings of Invisibility, and Protection: Studies on the Sources of the *Yvain* of Chrétien de Troyes," *Romanic Review*, V (1914); and Ferdinand Lot, "Le Chevalier au Lion: Comparaison avec une légende irlandaise," *Romania*, XXI (1892).

We have referred to these interpretations as extreme because to accept some of them one must be very strongly convinced of *detailed* Celtic derivation, or of great dependence upon Classical fable and myth. We do not believe there is sufficient evidence to *emphasize* either of these points of view, although the suggestions they have made are interesting from the viewpoint of comparative literature. On the realism in Chrétien see Pierre Jonin in *L'Information littéraire*, XVI (1964), 47–54. Raymond J. Cormier argues well for an eclectic approach (*Moyen-Age*, LXXV [1969], 87–94).

VII Celtic Origins

The Theory of Celtic origins began in 1869 with Rauch's *Die waelsche, franzoesische, und deutsche Bearbeitung der Iweinsage*. Arthur C. L. Brown became more extreme. As a graduate student in English at Harvard University he had been reading simultaneously with Fred Norris Robinson the Irish *Serglige Conchulainn* and with Edward S. Sheldon the Old French *Yvain*. He became aware of what seemed to him cogent parallels between the two. Heinrich Goosens in his *Uber Sage, Quelle, und Komposition des Chevaliers des Lyon des Crestien de Troyes* (diss. Paderborn, 1883) also supported the theory that the *Yvain* was a Celtic narrative told in French courts by Celtic minstrels. Franz Settegast (in *Zeitschrift für romanische Philologie*, XXII [1907], 60 ff., and XXXII (1917), 62 ff.) held that Byzantine history and the Cybele-Attis and Polyphemus legends were behind the *Yvain*.

VIII Adaptations

Around 1200 Hartmann von Aue translated Chrétien's *Yvain* into Middle High German. This *Iwein* is beautifully done and is quite free from obscurities and excessive diffuseness. By 1300 a Norse prose version appeared, and a second, more full, Norse version was made by 1316. This second version spread rather widely in Sweden and Denmark. There was also, in the fourteenth century, an English adaptation known as *Ywain and Gawain*. We have already discussed the *Mabinogion* Question—the relation to Chrétien of the Welsh prose *Owein and Lunete* preserved in the *Mabinogion* is greatly debated; we hold with Foerster that perhaps the Welsh romance went back ultimately to a text known to Chrétien.

Episodes from Chrétien's poem were used by later writers of Old French romance. The theme that most interested them was the Lion-Serpent episode; it was imitated in *Claris et Laris, Floriant et Florete, Sone de Nansay, Dame a la Lycorne, Gille de Chin,* and *Rigomer.*

CHAPTER 8

The Guillaume d'Angleterre

At the very beginning of this romance one reads:

Crestien wishes to tell a tale in rhyme, both simple and leonine,
without omitting or adding anything, straightforwardly. Provided he
keeps to the story he will not be deterred by anything. He will keep
to the straight road so that he can reach the end quickly. If you want
to find and seek out English tales—one which would be easily
believed because it is both true and attractive—you should go to
Bury-St. Edmund's. If someone wishes to prove this let him go himself and look. Crestien tells, who is accustomed to narrating, that
there was a king in England . . . (vss. 1–19)

At the close of the poem Chrétien adds: "This is the end of
this tale. I know nothing further and there is no more to add.
A friend of mine, Rogier the Attractive, who is well acquainted
with many fine men, told me this plot" (vss. 3306–10). Chrétien does not assert that he had visited the great Abbey of
Bury-St. Edmund's, but it is likely that he did. We assume
that his immediate source was a pious tale in Latin which Rogier
told him orally. No one can identify this friend, but Gröber
suggested that he was Rogier de Lisaïs.[1]

Many scholars refuse to admit that our Chrétien de Troyes was the Chrétien who names himself in this way; but there is little justification for their hesitation. More often than not our great poet signs himself only as Crestien. He mentions here that he is an active narrator, probably meaning that he was well known, and it is not easy to assume that there were several prominent writers of romance with the baptismal name Crestien. Gröber, Foerster, Wilmotte, Bezzola, and many others have accepted that the Chrétien who names himself in the *Cligés'* Prologue is the one who composed this *Guillaume d'Angleterre*. The prologue and signature which we have just translated have a familiar flavor, similar to the one we find in the *Erec*, the *Yvain*, and the *Lancelot*. Jean Frappier does not accept this attribution. He holds that the name Crestien was not uncommon, and therefore believes that another writer of romance with the same name could have been active in the area.

The principal manuscript is MS (P), B. N. 375, which contains also the *Erec et Enide* and the *Cligés*. There are twenty-nine items in this large composite manuscript which begins with the Latin *Apocalypse* and ends with nine miracles of Our Lady. Beginning with the sixth item the sequence is *Siege of Thebes*, *Roman de Troies*, *Siege of Athens*, *Congé* of Jehan Bodel, *Roman d'Alexandre*, Meaning of *La Mort Alexandre*, *Vengeance Alexandre*, Genealogy of the Dukes of Normandy, *Roman de Rou*, *Guillaume d'Angleterre* of Chrétien (folios 240–47), *Floire et Blanceflor*, *Roman de Blancandin*, *Cligés* of Chrétien, *Erec et Enide*, *Viellete*, *Ille et Galeron*, *Theophile* of Guillaume de Coincy, and so forth. Whether the arrangement of items was dictated by the individual who ordered the manuscript, or whether the sequence was according to someone else's whim, the train of thought is apparent: the *matière de Rome*, Alexander material, Normandy, the *Guillaume d'Angleterre*, *Floire et Blanceflore*, Chrétien's *Erec* and *Cligés*, the *Ille et Galeron*. We feel sure that the arranger associated the *Guillaume d'Angleterre* with the author of the *Erec* and the *Cligés*. He may even have assumed that *Floire et Blanceflor* was also by Chrétien. *Blancandin* is an adventure romance.

Another manuscript was discovered by Paul Meyer.[2] This is a fourteenth century manuscript in St. John's College, Cambridge, designated as C. Furthermore, in the Escorial Library near Madrid, in MS hI–13 of the Laurentius Collection, on folios 32 a-48 a, there is a Spanish prose version of the *Guillaume d'Angleterre*. Although the date of the extant manuscript is probably sixteenth century, the Spanish narrative may go back to the fourteenth. Hermann Knust printed this in his *Dos Obras Didácticas y Dos Leyendas sacadas de manuscritos de la Biblioteca del Escorial*.[3] The contents of this volume are *Flores de filosofía, De un caballero Placidas (Eustacio), La Estoria del rey Guillelme, Castigos y doctrinas,* and *Crónica del rey Guillermo*. Proximity makes it evident that the Placidas (Eustacius) legend was recognized as the source of the *Guillaume d'Angleterre*. Wendelin Foerster felt that this Spanish prose version was close enough to the Old French of Chrétien to be used for correcting the poem. He referred to it as Version E. This suggestion should be investigated further.

We follow Gröber in placing this romance between the *Yvain* and the *Conte dou Graal*.[4] We now give the outline of the plot as told by Chrétien:

I *Résumé*

Guillaume, king of England at Bristot (Bristol?), and his wife Gratiiene are childless in their first years of marriage. They pray faithfully, and in the sixth year she conceives. Just before Gratiiene's term is due, Guillaume, as he is rising for Matins, twice has a vision in which he is told to leave his land. His chaplain recommends that he arrange his accounts justly and distribute his wealth to the poor. He does this, but the vision occurs a third time and Guillaume is sure it comes from God. He sets off in secret, accompanied only by his wife, whom he cannot compel to remain behind.

They go through the woods for many days. They near the sea and make their bed on the rocks. There Guillaume helps deliver twin sons, whom he wraps in the tails of his cloak. He goes to a nearby harbor to beg food from the merchants, telling them of his wife's hunger; she is ready to eat the hands of her newborn sons. They scoff at Guillaume, who leads four of their number to Gratiiene. Unable to believe such a beautiful woman could have such an ill-clad husband, they propose to take her away in their ships. Guillaume reaches for his sword, but is stopped by the four, who then prepare a litter for Gratiiene. On parting they leave him a red purse with five besanz. He resolves to quit England by sea and, leaving one child on the rock, he takes the other to a boat. He returns to see the second child being carried off by a wolf, and unable to overtake them, he falls from fatigue. Upon reaching a highway the wolf is stoned by merchants and drops the child. A merchant named Gonselin adopts him and they come to the ship, wherein they find the second son, who is adopted by a merchant called Fouchier. The king awakens and finds his second child gone. He returns to the rock to take the money-purse, but it is snatched from him by an eagle. Guillaume believes that God is angered by his covetousness, and laments the state to which it has reduced him.

Wandering aimlessly, he comes upon a group of merchants eating in a meadow. They agree to take him in their ship to Galloway. There he is hired into household service by a rich bourgeois, and rises to a position of authority.

Gratiiene, meanwhile, has been taken into the household of Gleolais, the lord of Sterling, who is left childless when his wife dies. He has loved Gratiiene since first he saw her, and now wishes to wed her. She tells him that this would be to his shame, for she is of base birth, and furthermore had fled nun's vows to become a wanton woman. He wishes her nonetheless, and thus trapped she agrees to the marriage, on condition that he will not touch her before a year is out, for she pretends to have a third year of penance to complete. (Later we learn that this ruse preserves her honor, since the lord dies within the year.)

The sons, Lovel (<*loup*) and Marin (<*mer*), have meanwhile grown to be healthy lads of ten, and are fast friends although they do not realize they are brothers. Their intimate associations with a low-class milieu has not affected their basically noble natures, and when their stepfathers wish to make them furriers (*peletier*) they rebel. Fouchier vilifies Marin and tells how he found him in the boat. He gives him the piece of cloak in which he was wrapped, and Marin flees the town in shame. Lovel also learns the circumstances of his discovery, but recognizes his stepfather's love and makes peace with him. Before setting out into the world he is outfitted and given two horses and a squire, Rodain.

Leaving the town Lovel comes upon Marin, who tells of his quarrel with his stepfather. They join company and kill a buck (*daim*), then come to a clear spring and stream, beside which they see a newly-built shed. Inside they find only a sparrow on a perch. They decide to pass the night there and prepare to eat their buck. The local gamekeeper appears and wishes to have them severely punished. He is bribed, however, and the next morning intercedes in their favor before the king of Caithness, who takes them into his household.

Twenty-four years have passed since the separation of the family, and Guillaume has risen to such a position of trust that the bourgeois sends his two sons with Guillaume on his ship to Bristol, where his nephew has become king. At the market there Guillaume recognizes a hunting horn from his own castle, and the youth who has it tells him of the sacking of the castle shortly after their king's disappearance. Guillaume's nephew hears of the presence in the market of a merchant who resembles closely his lost uncle. He comes to ask him to be his seneschal, but Guillaume refuses and soon sets sail.

A storm batters his ship for three days and takes it to a strange land. The port tax is high: the lady of the castle may choose any one item from the cargo, but the rest can be sold at good profit. The lady, who has been sole ruler of the land since the death of her husband shortly after their marriage, comes with veiled face and demands only Gratiiene's ring, which Guillaume has kept all these years. He reluctantly gives it to her and is invited to the manor, where at supper he realizes that the veiled lady is Gratiiene. Still at table, Guillaume imagines he is on a deer-hunt and cries out. The guests laugh, but Gratiiene takes him in her arms and promises to make his dream a reality.

That very evening Guillaume follows a deer across the river which divides Gratiiene's land from that of her enemy, the king of Caithness. After killing the deer he sounds his horn and when two enemy knights appear he realizes his trespass. To prevent their slaying him he tells them of his royalty and of his sad adventures. The purse which the eagle had snatched drops from the sky and the two knights recognize that this is indeed

their father. They return to the king of Caithness and plan
to make peace with their neighbor, who they learn is their own
mother.

Meanwhile, believing her husband dead, Gratiiene raises an
army to go into Caithness to avenge him. On the way they
meet Guillaume and his sons, and the family is joyfully reunited in Sterling. The sons send for their stepfathers, whom
they present to their true parents. After nine days, Guillaume and his family set sail and arrive at the rock where
the boys were born. Word spreads of their arrival in England,
and the nephew comes gladly to return the crown to its rightful possessor. Guillaume, back in London, rewards the bourgeois of Galloway who had protected him, and marries his sons
to the daughters of two rich counts.

II Source

It has been recognized by the compiler of the Escorial manuscript, and by all modern critics, that the pious tale which was
known to Chrétien had its basis in the Placidas-Eustacius legend.
We retell this briefly.

Placidas, a pagan, was a high military officer in Trajan's army.
As he was chasing a stag the animal turned to face him and
he saw a crucifix on its breast. The stag spoke and said that
he had come to convert Placidas. He asked whether Placidas
would rather have misfortunes now or after death. Placidas chose
the immediate time. The stag, who was really Christ, said that
he would make of him a Job. Placidas and his wife were baptized by the Bishop of Rome; Placidas took the name Eustacius,
his wife became Theospita, and his two infant sons were called
Agapius and Thespilus. When the family returned to their es-
tates they found everything ruined by pestilence and robbery.
They determined to go to Egypt. But they had no money to
pay passage; the captain kept the wife, while Eustacius and
his sons were thrown into the sea. Later, when the father was
crossing a river with one son, the other was stolen by a lion;
then the remaining one was taken by a wolf. Eustacius went
to Badyssus where he worked as a laborer for *fifteen years*.
A shepherd saved the son from the lion; the other had been

taken from the wolf by a ploughman. Meanwhile, Theospita had escaped from the advances of the seaman and become a seamstress. Trajan's enemies were pressing him sorely and he sent far and wide to find Placidas-Eustacius. He was discovered, thanks to a prominent scar, and returned to his military post. In his bodyguard were his two sons, who were soldiers. While camping they lodged with a lady, who was Theospita. They recognized one another; Theospita went to tell Placidas-Eustacius, and recognized him. All was well after the reunion. But then Hadrian, a pagan emperor, succeeded to the throne. He persecuted the Christians. The members of the family were thrown to a lion who refused to hurt them. Then they were placed inside a white-hot brazen ox. They died, but their bodies remained unscorched and they were given Christian burial.

This narrative and other variants are discussed very effectively by Gordon Hall Gerould.[5] The *Guillaume d'Angleterre* by Chrétien is there mentioned as the earliest extant derivative; others are the English *Ysumbras*, the Spanish *Caballero de Cifar*, and various versions in German. Professor Gerould does not mention the Old French *Jourdain de Blaivie*. The tale is also in the *Gesta Romanorum*, of about 1450. The relation of this pious tale to the two actual SS. Placidus and Eutichius, brothers, who were said to have been martyred by Saracen Spanish pirates near Messina, has not been established: but the similarity of names is rather convincing. These saints were said to be disciples of St. Benedict; they were sent to Messina to establish there the Church of St. John the Baptist. Their legend, false in most details, was written by Peter the Deacon at Monte Cassino in the twelfth century. It is the *Passio S. Placidi*. This tale of Placidas-Eustacius is classified by Stith Thompson as a folk theme, with the designation N251.[6]

We have good reason to suspect that Chrétien de Troyes, in the heart of Champagne, was interested in Byzantine material. The *Cligés* shows much evidence of this—and we consider it of some significance that the *Guillaume d'Angleterre* is placed so close to the *Cligés* in B. N. MS 375. (The *Floire et Blanceflor* is also Byzantine in inspiration, and perhaps also the *Roman de Blancandin*.) We have stated elsewhere that the court at Troyes had strong Byzantine interests and associations. Henri I of Troyes was knighted by Emperor Manuel Comnenos, and the German emperor, close at hand, maintained connections with Manuel. We suspect that Clairvaux was also a center for some of this Greek interest; but this is difficult to formulate. The inspiration for retelling this pious tale in French verse (for the first time?) could have come from the environment at Troyes.

Because he was directing his narratives towards a feudal audience, Chrétien, of course, placed the new narrative within a Western feudal mould. This was a subconscious association. To be explained, however, is the geographical location of the tale in Bristol, Galloway, Sterling, and Caithness.[7] These are place names that Chrétien could have learned while in England (assuming that he never actually went to Scotland), but why did he use them? We can only guess. We have suggested that the sources which furnished the Glastonbury entourage with many of the Arthurian themes had some association with Scotland. We assume that the "Ford Perilous" was the Solway Firth which separated England (Carlisle, etc.) from the land of the Picts and the Scots, that is Galloway. Chrétien deliberately wanted to picture the carrying off of his protagonists into a strange land, the equivalent of the Egypt of the Placidas legend. Familiar to him by name—but perhaps very strange—was the land of the Scots. His geography was far from perfect. Caithness is quite far to the north; Sterling cannot be designated as a seaport; Galloway was only a name to him. Bristol, on the other hand, he knew. This was very much a seaport and it was from there that most vessels bound for Ireland began their voyages.

In recent years a number of articles have been written on the *Guillaume d'Angleterre*, mostly to ascertain the processes which went on in the poet's subconcious mind.[8] These efforts may be justified, but the main issues are as we have outlined them. Chrétien laid his action in a land about which he probably had few details. As depicted by Jocelin in his life of Abbot Samson of Bury-St. Edmunds, the Scot of the twelfth century was a rough and ready character who liked to take off his shoes, who carried a staff, and who swore big oaths.[9] Chrétien's view could not have been more favorable. Certainly if we are justified in equating the Isles with Galloway—across the Solway—in Chrétien's *Conte dou Graal*, we may assume that Chrétien's concept of Scotland was along these lines.[10]

CHAPTER 9

The Conte dou Graal, or Perceval

I Résumé

In springtime, a young man (who will someday know his
name to be Perceval) leaves the manor of his widowed mother
to visit with their peasants (the harrowers) in the field. In
the wood he meets five knights whom, in innocence, he mistakes
for God and his angels. When their spokesman asks if he has
seen five other knights with three maidens, he does not answer
and instead asks the knight about the use of his lance,
shield, and hauberk. ·The boy leads the five to the mountain,
where a herdsman informs them that those they seek have passed
by that day.

The knights continue their journey. The young man returns
home and tells this adventure to his mother. She is sorely grieved
that he has learned of knighthood, since his father and two
brothers had died in the service of chivalry. She realizes, however,
that he must go to Arthur's court, and counsels him to be true
in the service of women, to frequent only noble companions,
and to pray for honor and a worthy end. As he rides off he
sees his mother fall as if dead, but urges his horse onward.
The morning of the second day he sees a magnificent tent in

a meadow, and thinks it to be a temple of God. Within he finds a sleeping girl, and in accord with his mother's advice he wishes to serve her. On awakening she is startled to find herself alone with him, and insists he leave. But he naively kisses her seven times, then forces her ring from her finger. Content with his actions, he leaves her weeping, and before setting off, eats the food he finds in her tent. Her knight returns and vows to uphold his honor, believing that his lady willingly gave her ring, her kisses, and the food.

With directions from a charcoal-seller, the young protagonist arrives at Arthur's court after encountering the Red Knight, who has challenged Arthur's lands. He enters the king's presence and learns that this Red Knight has just stolen Arthur's golden cup, after spilling wine on the queen. Refusing to dismount, he asks to be knighted and granted the arms of the Red Knight. Kay mocks him, and slaps a young girl who smiles and foretells the young knight's greatness. The youth rides out to capture the Red Knights' arms, and slays him with a simple weapon, a dart. He removes the armor, and rides on his way after returning Arthur's cup and vowing to avenge the young girl. He reaches a castle where he receives lodging for the night. There Gornemant de Gorhaut teaches him to use the arms he has won and gives him new clothing which he reluctantly dons. In the morning he sets off to visit his mother, after listening to Gornemant's advice: a knight must be merciful, reflective, provident, and pious, and must not always quote his mother.

A day's journey brings him to Biaurepaire. A pale maiden answers his knock, and four sergeants lead him through a ruined town to a place where he is offered simple lodgings by two gentlement and the beautiful and richly-robed Blancheflor, niece of Gornemant. After a meager dinner he retires to sleep, but is soon awakened by Blancheflor's tears. She has come to his bed to tell him that all but fifty of her three hundred and ten knights have been killed or imprisoned by Engygneron, the seneschal of King Clamedeu des Illes, who has besieged the town for a winter and a summer. Tomorrow the town will be surrendered, and she will kill herself, unless he saves them. They lie side by side. In the morning the young man defeats Engygneron and sends him as prisoner to the girl whom Kay had slapped and he had promised to avenge.

Clamedeu learns of this defeat and hastens to attack Biaurepaire. He is repulsed on the first day, and plans to lay siege to the town. However, a good wind blows a merchant vessel laden with food into the harbor, and Clamedeu realizes that his only hope is to challenge the young knight to single combat. The next morning the hero defeats him and exacts the same tribute as that given previously to the seneschal; in addition he obtains the freedom of the prisoners Clamedeu has taken from Biaurepaire. He then takes leave of Blancheflor to go visit his mother.

Seeking a place to lodge, he comes to a river. He sees a boat with two men fishing, using for bait little fish slightly larger than minnows. Since he cannot cross the river, one of the men directs him to a beautiful castle which he finds after some difficulty. He crosses the castle drawbridge and is met by four servitors who give him a scarlet mantle. He proceeds through a series of loges and then enters the hall, which is perfectly square.

In the center of the hall an old man clad in black with purple edging, is resting on his elbow by a fire. Perceval joins him on his couch. A squire enters with a sword sent by the old man's niece, to be given to anyone he may choose. The sword is handed to the hero, for whom it has been destined, and it is noted that there are only three of these swords and that no more will be made. He admires the sword, hands it to a valet to keep for him, then sits again beside the old man, observing the Grail procession. A young man enters with a white lance, and Perceval observes a single drop of blood running from the blade tip to the bearer's hand. Two more youths enter, bearing ten-branched candlesticks, and with them a damsel holding in her hands a golden Grail set with precious stones. The light of the Grail eclipses that of the candles. They are followed by a second damsel with a silver plate. Perceval is curious, but remembers Gornemant's advice and asks no questions. The procession passes out of the hall, and an ivory table is brought in and placed upon trestles of strange and rare wood. They are served venison, on whole white wafers, from a silver platter and at each course the damsel with the Grail returns and passes between the couch and the fire. This feast is followed by fruit, and then they retire.

The next morning the castle appears deserted. The young knight finds his arms and goes forth. The drawbridge pulls up mysteriously under him, and he is only saved by his horse's mighty leap. He soon encounters a girl weeping over the headless body of her knight, whom she will not leave until he is buried. She asks the knight if he has spent the night at the castle of the Fisher King. He replies affirmatively. She tells him that his host and the fisherman who had directed him to the castle were the same person and that his host has been wounded in both hips. She chides him for not having inquired the meaning of the Grail procession, for if he had the king would have been healed. She also tells him that he is in a state of sin because he let his mother die of grief at his departure, and declares that the sword he carries will fail him. It can only be repaired by its maker, Triboet, who lives by the lake below Cothoatre. She asks him his name, and he guesses, not knowing whether or not he is right: the name is Perceval.

Perceval sets out again. Soon he meets the girl from whom he had taken the ring; by now she is in a most sorry state because of the jealousy of her knight, Orgueilleus de la Lande. Perceval identifies himself as the cause of her grief and defeats her knight, but not without breaking the sword he has been given by the Fisher King. He has mercy on Orgueilleus and sends him to Arthur, who is anxious to learn Perceval's identity and determines to go with his full retinue to seek him out.

Perceval meanwhile loses himself in contemplation of the blood of a wounded goose on white snow, which reminds him of the rosy cheeks of his lady, Blancheflor. Kay and Sagremor attempt to distract him and bring him by force to Arthur, but both are defeated. Kay has an arm and leg broken. Gawain then succeeds through kindness where the others have failed with arms, and Arthur welcomes Perceval after learning his name.

A hideous damsel on a yellow mule arrives on the third day who denounces Perceval for not daring to ask the import of the Grail procession, which would have healed the Fisher King. Because of his failure, ladies will lose husbands, lands will be destroyed, girls will be orphaned. The hideous damsel will return that night to Chastel Orgueillous, but announces an adventure before she goes: a knight must rescue a maiden from the besieged town of Montesclaire and win the sword with strange hangings. At this moment Guigambresil arrives and accuses Gawain of killing his lord. Thereupon, Gawain sets out to defend his honor. He meets with Melian de Lis, who is intent upon winning the elder daughter of his tutor Tibaut de Tintagueil in a tournament. Melian shows great prowess, but Tibaut's youngest daughter assures her elder sister that there is a greater knight present: Gawain. This angers the elder sister, and her ladies mock Gawain, whom they think to be only a merchant since he has not fought that day. At night he enters the city to take lodging with Garin the vavassor. The lord, urged by his elder daughter, goes to confiscate the arms of this "merchant," who tells him he could not fight because he has not yet righted Guigambresil's insult. Tibaut grants him safe passage, but Gawain stays one more day to defend the honor of the youngest daughter.

The following day Gawain comes to a castle where, before leaving on a hunt, the king recommends him to his sister. When Gawain begins to kiss her, they are overseen by a vavassor, who says that Gawain has killed the girl's father. The townspeople assail Gawain in the tower. Guigambresil arrives to explain the situation to the king, who chooses to protect Gawain now that he has given him lodging. His vavassor suggests an honorable solution: the king will release Gawain if he promise to return within one year with the Bleeding Lance, for it has been written that the kingdom of Logres is destined to be destroyed by it.

Perceval, meanwhile, has wandered about for five years, forgetting God completely. On Good Friday he meets three knights and their ladies dressed as penitents who induce him to visit a saintly hermit. This hermit tells Perceval that he was not able to ask the meaning of the Grail procession because he had sinned in letting his mother die of grief. He explains to Perceval that in the chamber beyond the one where the Fisher King received his guest was a being who was fed on the Grail bread (*oiste*) alone, not on any diet of fish. This being, who had not left the chamber for a long while, is the brother of the hermit and of Perceval's mother, and the father of the Fisher King. The hermit then absolves Perceval from the guilt of his mother's death.

After Gawain's escape from the town, he comes in the late

afternoon upon a girl weeping beneath an oak for her wounded knight. This knight warns Gawain of impending danger, for no knight can return from beyond the boundary of Galvoie (Galloway). Gawain rides until he sees a maiden seated beneath an elm. She knows he has come to carry her off, but warns him of the ill-adventure and shame this will entail. She sends him dismounted into the meadow to fetch her palfrey, and despite several warnings he brings it across the bridge to her. He then leads the maiden to where the first girl is still weeping. He applies herbs to her knight's wounds and he, in order that he may go confess his sins, has Gawain seize a nag (*ronchin*) from a passing squire. The knight reveals that he is Gawain's enemy Greoreas; he steals Gawain's horse Gringalet, and leaves the nag behind. Gawain, still leading the distraught maiden upon her palfrey, comes to a wide river on the other side of which he sees a mighty fortress. The *evil* maiden invites him to cross with her in a boat they find, but Gawain sees the nephew of Greoreas approaching on Gringalet. Though he has but a nag, he refuses to flee and manages to recover his steed. When Gawain returns to the river he finds neither boat nor maiden.

A boatman comes to ferry Gawain across the river, and gives him lodging for the night. He tells Gawain that the fortress houses two queens and many maidens and knights, but that they cannot inherit, be married, or knighted until some pure knight break an astrologer's (*clerc sage d'astronomie*) spell. The two pass by a man with an ornate artificial leg and arrive at the ivory and ebony gates of the palace. Inside Gawain sees a marvelous bed (li Lis de la Merveille). When he ignores the boatman's warning not to sit upon it, he is assailed by arrows from all sides, but lives to kill the lion which attacks him next. He is then hailed by all as their prince, and warned he should never again leave the fortress. A queen comes and inquires about King Arthur's court; they dine; Gawain sleeps that night in the marvelous bed. The next morning he sees an armed knight approaching with the maiden who had left him. In spite of the queen's warning, he goes back across the river to meet them.

He captures her knight, Orgueilleus del Passage a Estroite Voie, but she will not yield to Gawain until he passes the Perilous Ford (*Guez Perillous*), which he does with some difficulty. On the other side he meets Guiromelan who has been abandoned by the evil maiden. He tells Gawain her name: Orgueilleuse de Logres. Gawain inquires about the fortress and Guiromelan is hesitant to answer until Gawain tells him of his adventures there. He then informs Gawain that the queens who live in the Roche de Canguin are Gawain's mother, his sister Clarissans, and Ygerne, the mother of Arthur. Not recognizing his interlocutor, Guiromelans admits to hating both Gawain (who has killed his cousin) and Gawain's father (who has killed his father). Gawain identifies himself, and a duel is arranged to be held in seven days. He returns to Orgueilleuse de Logres, who tells him she became so inhospitable after Guiromelan killed her knight and tried to force her love. Gawain brings her to Roche de Canguin. Revealing his name only to a valet, he sends him to Arthur, and Chrétien's version of the *roman* ends here as the messenger arrives at the king's court in Orquenie.

In his continuation of the *Conte dou Graal,* Gerbert de Montreuil informs us why Chrétien did not proceed further than verse 9234 with this wonderful story: "Chrestien de Troie, who began the story of the Perceval told all this—but Death overtook him and did not let him bring it to an end" (Gerbert Continuation, vss. 6984–87).

II *Manuscripts and Editions.*

Perceval is preserved in fifteen manuscripts: Paris, B. N. fonds francais 794 (A); Bern, Bibliothèque de la Ville 354 (B); Clermont-Ferrand, Bibliothèque de la Ville 248 (C); Edinburgh, National Library of Scotland 19.1.5 (E); Florence, Biblioteca Riccardiana 2943 (F); London, Heralds' College, Arundel 14 (H); London, British Museum Additional 36614; Montpellier, Bibliothèque de la Faculté de Medecine H. 249 (M); Mons, Bibliothèque Publique 331–206 (P); Paris, B. N. fonds francais 1429 (Q); Paris, B. N. fonds frç. 1450 (R); Paris B. N. fonds frç. 1453 (S); Paris, B. N. fonds frç. 12576 (T); Paris, B. N. fonds frç. 12577 (U); Paris, B. N. nouvelles acquisitions françaises 6614 (V). MS. B. N. 794, written by the copyist Guiot early in the thirteenth century, has been preferred by Mario Roques for his editions of the Chrétien romances: "He who copied this is named Guiot; his lodging is permanently in front of Notre Dame del Val" (*Cligés*, vss. 6663–64). Beaulieux gives credit to this professional copyist for some of the Old French spelling system which was developed in the twelfth and thirteenth centuries. Beaulieux reminds us that Guiot was copying not very long after the death of Chrétien.[1]

The first printing of the *Perceval*, a modernization of Chrétien's text, was made in 1530: the *Tresplaisante et recreative hystoire du Trespreulx et vaillant chevalier Perceval le galloys, jadis chevalier de la Table ronde, lequel acheva les adventures du Sainct Graal, etc. translatee de ryme en prose de l'ancien auteur Chrétien de Troyes et de Gautier de Denet son continuateur* (Imprimé a Paris, pour Jehan Sainct Denys et Jehan Longis. . . . et fut achevé de imprimer le premier jour de Septembre. Lan mil cinq cens trente. Infol). This edition survives in only one copy; we have taken the title from Brunet, *Manuel du libraire*.[2] We are not absolutely certain of its contents or of its relationship to the known manuscripts.

Charles Potvin published six volumes in 1866–71 entitled *Perceval le Gallois ou le Conte du Graal publié d'apres les manuscrits originaus* (Mons: Dequesne-Masquillier), for the Société des Philologues belges (Mons). Chrétien's poem is in volumes II and III. This contains also the Continuations, the Elucidation and Bliocadran Prologues (from the Mons MS), and the *Perlesvaus*. Some of the material is abbreviated. This edition represents the first entry of the *Conte dou Graal* into the world of scholarship—the beginning of the puzzle. Gottfried Baist prepared for his students an edition of the *Perceval* in 1909, based upon B. N. MS 794.[3]

Alfons Hilka was the next editor. His *Der Percevalroman von Christian von Troyes*[4] made use of manuscript materials left by Baist. This served for many years as the standard edition; but the best edition is now the one made by William Roach from MS T in 1959.[5] Professor Roach, since 1949, has been in the process of publishing the Continuators of Chrétien.

III   Continuations and Later Versions

These Continuators, who added directly to Chrétien's *Perceval*, must be kept in mind. The first, an anonymous writer whom

we are accustomed to referring to as the Pseudo-Wauchier, carried on the adventures of Gawain, after Chrétien, through verse
21916. Another, who names himself as Gauchier de Dourdan,
or Gautier de Doulens (according to the manuscript), was identified by Paul Meyer as Wauchier de Denain.[6] He brought the
action down through verse 34934. Still another, named Manecier,
continued Wauchier as far as verse 45379; he wrote for Countess
Jeanne of Flanders. A certain Gerbert, possibly Gerbert de
Montreuil—author of the *Roman de la Violette*—also continued
Wauchier, independent of Manecier, writing some 15,000 verses.
One episode in this Gerbert Continuation is especially important
—the *Tristan Menestrel*.[7] The last of these Continuations were
added in the first quarter of the thirteenth century.

Some time between 1180 and 1199, a knight named Robert
of Boron composed a history of the Holy Grail. According to
this narrative, Joseph of Arimathea, one of Pilate's soldiers,
obtains from his master the Body of Christ and the Vessel of
the Last Supper. As the Body is washed, the Sacred Blood flows
again and is caught in the vessel. Joseph is imprisoned. Christ
appears to him, bringing the Vessel, and stating that this shall
be entrusted to three persons only: Joseph, Bron, and Bron's
grandson. Joseph remains in the prison until rescued by Ves-
pasian. Bron (Hebron) is the husband of Joseph's sister. The
voice of the Holy Ghost bids Joseph prepare a Table, a counterpart of the Last Supper. Bron will supply a fish. This is the
Grail Table. Those who are not sinners find delight when seated
there. One persistent sinner, Moyses, is swallowed up in the
earth. One of the twelve sons of Bron is Alain; from him shall
come an heir who will keep the Vessel. In the meantime, Bron,
known as the Rich Fisher, is given the Grail and then goes
westward to the vale of Avaron, or Avalon. This Grail henceforth is the symbol of the Sacrament—it means the establish-
ment of Ecclesia, the church, in place of Sinagoga, the Old
Covenant.

Many scholars feel that the only connection between Chrétien
and Robert of Boron is that they both drew upon the same
sources, now lost. But it is probable that Robert knew Chrétien's
Perceval, to the extent that he took from it the concepts of
the Grail Vessel and of the Fisher King. Robert also wrote a
Merlin, and a prose account of the Quest of the Grail which

is commonly referred to as the *Didot Perceval*. We are not concerned further with the works of Robert of Boron in this book on Chrétien. Suffice it to say that Robert of Boron, and others, almost immediately after Chrétien, interpreted his meaning in terms of Christian mysticism.

Another Grail prose narrative of the last decade of the twelfth century, the *Perlesvaus*, associates the Grail with the Abbey of Glastonbury.

IV *Vulgate Romances and Similar Compilations*

In addition to the Continuations, which were attached in sequence to the actual text of Chrétien's *Conte dou Graal*, and to the *Joseph of Arimathea* and the *Perlesvaus*, there are the so-called Vulgate Romances which are *prose* compositions of a very different style. These were written independently between 1215 and 1230, consisting of five branches: the *Prose Lancelot*, the *Queste del Saint Greal*, the *Mort Artu* (these three form a first group)—and then the *Estoire del Saint Graal* and the *Estoire de Merlin* (consisting of a prose version of Robert of Boron's *Merlin* and a pseudo-chronicle of Arthur's early wars). We have already spoken of the *Prose Lancelot*. The order we give for these is more or less according to date of composition. If the five are arranged in order of their position in a connected narrative the sequence would be: 4–5–1–2–3. These prose works, which form a tremendously long account, have been falsely attributed to a single author, Walter Mapes, and are thus sometimes called the Pseudo-Walter Mapes Cycle. Not very long after their composition the same material was handled again by other writers, in an attempt to feature King Arthur more prominently. This collection is referred to as the Pseudo-Robert of Boron Cycle, or the Post-Vulgate *Roman de Graal*. It contained a version of the *Estoire del Graal*, a prose version of Robert of Boron's *Merlin*, the *Suite du Merlin* (or *Huth Merlin*), a remodeled *Queste*, and a reworked *Mort Artu*.

A vast prose compilation known as the *Prose Tristan* was compiled to match the *Prose Lancelot* (see above). Among its many manuscripts it is possible to distinguish a First Version (much the shorter), and a Second Version (known as the Cyclic

Tristan or Common version). The First Version is attributed to a Missire Luce de Gaut—the second to a Missire Helie de Borron. In these the knight Tristan is a full-fledged member of Arthur's Court. Both narratives claim to be translated from Latin. We assume that the original source from which these two extant forms derived was written between 1226 and 1235. It has been lost.

We can reconstruct the Pseudo-Robert of Boron Cycle only from sections found here and there. The *Huth Merlin* is fairly well preserved in B. M. Add. 38117 (the Huth manuscript) and in Cambridge Univ. Libr. MS Add. 7071. A small section of the *Suite du Merlin* is in a fifteenth-century compilation (B.N. f.frç. 112, Livre II, ff. 17b–58b). The remodeled *Queste* can be appreciated from certain manuscripts of the second *Prose Tristan*, from the Spanish and Portuguese *Demandas del Santo Graal*, and from the *Queste* versions in B. N. 112 and 343. Two brief fragments of the *Mort Artu* are in B.N. F. fr. 340, ff. 205a–207c. The Spanish *Demanda* gives a complete version of this in Chapters CCCXCI-CCCCLV; the Portuguese *Demanda* has this Chapter II, paragraphs 626–706. A section of the *Suite de Merlin,* hitherto unidentified, has been published by Fanni Bogdanow under the title *La Folie Lancelot* from B. N. f.fr. 12599 and B.N. f.fr. 112, Livre III. Mme Bogdanow will publish in the "Société des Anciens Textes" series a critical edition of the Pseudo-Robert of Boron *Queste* and *Mort Artu,* as far as they can be reconstituted.

V   *Christian Interpretation*

It is quite evident that writers who followed soon after Chrétien thought of his Grail narrative as having Christian inspiration. Therefore, in the nineteenth century, when modern scholars first came to be concerned with the interpretation of Chrétien's Grail, it was natural for this Christian explanation to take the lead. A good summary of this has been given by James Douglas Bruce in his *Evolution of Arthurian Romance.*[8] The proponents of this Christian explanation contend that the Grail was a vessel of Grace—that those who partake of the Grail Feast do so spiritually. Writing of the *Joseph of Arimathea* of Robert of Boron, Bruce says:

The interpretation of the events of the Old Testament as a sort of allegorical adumbration of those of the New Testament was still a vital element in the Biblical exegesis of the age [twelfth century], and so there was no new departure in Robert's employment of this method. It is to be observed too that in no other period of the Church has the doctrine of Transubstantiation been so immediately the centre of theological interest and discussions as in the latter part of the twelfth century and the early decades of the thirteenth.[9]

(But it never occurred to Bruce and his associates in this Christian explanation theory to look specifically for this same Sinago-ga-Ecclesia motif in Chrétien's *Conte dou Graal.*)

For those who accept this Christian meaning theory, the principal points in Chrétien's poem are these:

1. The Grail vessel and the Question that should be asked.
2. The Great Fool Motif, which is prevalent in folklore.
3. The Arthurian setting.
4. The character of Perceval and the concept of a Quest, which were devised by Chrétien himself.
5. Motifs which were repeated from Chrétien's earlier works
6. The Grail Procession as the Procession of the Mass according to the Byzantine Rite. It is not necessary for this to take place only in a church. A woman carrying the Host is possible in the East.
7. The Fisher King, who is Christ Himself; the Being in the inner room who partakes of the Host is the Holy Ghost.
8. Glastonbury is not essential as a location; Avalon merely means "Land of the West."

This sort of interpretation, which we find quite satisfying, does *not* explain, however, the great good that will come to the Fisher King's (Christ's) land by the asking of the Question (see the remarks of the Hideous Damsel). Does it mean that all the World will be converted to Christ, once the meaning of the Procession is explained to Perceval? Who then is Perceval? The Christian theorists attach no special significance to the name itself.

VI *Maurice Wilmotte*

Maurice Wilmotte (*Le Poéme du Graal et ses auteurs* [Paris, 1930]) believed with Bruce that the book furnished by Philip

of Flanders to Chrétien contained a history of the Relic of the
Precious Blood, together with some account of a virtuous knight
who was sufficiently worthy to keep it. He thought that Robert
of Boron and a certain Guiot, mentioned in the *Parzifal* of
Wolfram von Eschenbach, had already used this account. The
Grail Quest was a "quest" to find out who was the best knight.
Wilmotte thought that Arthur reflected the English King Henry
II, and that the episode at the court of Guigambresil reflected
local rioting in Flanders, which Chrétien could have observed
while with Philip of Flanders. Above all, Wilmotte insisted that
Chrétien did not stop writing at verse 9198 (or 10601, depend-
ing upon the manuscript), as is generally accepted. He attributed
to Chrétien much of what is ordinarily assigned to the Continuators. It is possible that Chrétien was intending, in the latter
part of his poem, to make Gawain the one who would restore
the prosperity of the Land. Wilmotte is sure that Chrétien finished
his work on this poem before the Pact of Gisors, between
Henry II and Philip Augustus, on May 14, 1181.

VII *Stefan Hofer*

The highest point in the Christian explanation of the Grail
theme is reached by Stefan Hofer in his *Chrétien de Troyes*
(*loc cit*). Making considerable use of Konrad Burdach's *Der
Gral* (Stüttgart, 1938), he concludes that the mysterious book
which Count Philip showed to Chrétien was a book on the
Passion Relics of Jerusalem, in which there were ceremonial
descriptions according to the Byzantine Rite. Count Philip's
mother was a daughter of Foulque, king of Jerusalem. Philip
persuaded Chrétien to treat in romance form certain mystical
reflections of the late twelfth century. The Lance, with the Blood
of Christ dripping upon the hand of the soldier, was considered
the palladium or protective symbol of Western knighthood—
victory in Christ. The Grail was the Chalice, of heavenly beauty,
containing the Sacred Host; the *tailleor* was the paten, which
does not in this instance bear the Host. The purpose of this
Grail poem was to show that worldly knighthood, based upon
courtesy and worldly love, must give way to a knighthood of
Charity and Compassion. The poet assumes the existence of

a Grail Castle which is the opposite of Arthur's court. It has knights, squires, and ladies, and a magnificent host into whose company Perceval will eventually gain admission when he has achieved atonement with God. Hofer is not completely sure about the Gawain adventures. They depict, of course, knighthood without this great Compassion; perhaps they were originally a separate poem. It is to be noted that Chrétien places the Bleeding Lance before the Chalice. Robert of Boron's *Estoire dou Graal* would be the source of Chrétien's Fisher King; but Chrétien made little use of this work. Their sources were similar but different. Robert is not concerned with the Bleeding Lance. For Chrétien, the Lance and the Grail together were the symbol of one who fights for God, who follows the instructions as set forth by the Hermit. Hofer dates the Chrétien poem in 1180–87. He believes that Count Philip brought the book on the Sacred Relics back with him from the Holy Land in 1177–78 and that Chrétien joined the Count's Court in 1179–80.

VIII *Jean Frappier*

Jean Frappier (*Chrétien de Troyes, loc. cit.*) admits readily that Chrétien has Christianized some Celtic fairy themes. He does not believe that a grail has any association with a chalice, and he cites passages from the Old French Alexander romance, the *Girart de Roussillon,* and Helinandus de Froidmont to prove this. (Some of us counter that the likening of the dish, or *catinus,* used by Our Lord at the Last Supper, to a chalice containing the Host has been widespread. The lovely set of silver vessels found in the house of Menander at Pompei—now in the Naples Museum—has several such *catini.* They are not platters, flat round dishes, nor is a medieval *escuele,* which Helinandus describes as "broad and somewhat deep," a flat dish. A grail was a show dish of some kind.) M. Frappier believes that Chrétiens' grail was a food producing vessel, with analogues among the Celts. He does not agree that the Sacred Lance could have been thought of as bringing destruction. He suggests that the Being in the inner room may be a later accretion. The Grail bearer could have been a Celtic fairy in some earlier form of the legend. Frappier admits that the Gawain episodes were probably intended to contrast in some way with those of Perceval. But, especially significant, he agrees with Mario Roques that a miniature in the *Hortus deliciarum* manuscript, depicting the Sinagoga-Ecclesia allegory, expresses an idea which could have influenced the form of the Grail Procession as presented by Chrétien (*op. cit.,* p. 192).

M. Frappier has made a praiseworthy attempt to reconcile some of the differences among scholars on this subject; but he does not accept symbolism to any extent. Chrétien, he says, was above all a great literary artist who replaced stylized descriptions by eloquent details which were admirably appropriate to the narrative. (For what purpose did Chrétien give the color of a Sinagoga-Ecclesia procession to a fairy procession from Celtic sources?)

There is a different angle on the Christian theory in Helen Adolf's *Visio Pacis, An Attempt at an Inner History of the Grail Legend* (University Park: Pennsylvania State University Press, 1960). For her, "the Grail legend is the fruit of the Crusades." The Grail stands for the Holy Sepulcher, the Holy City. The Fisher King is Baldwin IV, the leper king of Jerusalem, and the Being in the Inner room may be the spirit of Godfrey of Bouillon. She believes that Robert of Boron's *Joseph of Arimathea* was written to console the West for the fall of Jerusalem.

In addition to these so-called Christian interpretations, five other views have been proposed in the past seventy-five years: Ritualistic origin, Celtic origins, Oriental sources, Heterodox Christian origin, and Judeo-Christian origin.

IX *The Ritualist Theory*

The Ritualist theory was first proposed by Karl Simrock in 1842.[10] It became well known through Jessie L. Weston's *Legend of Sir Perceval*[11] and *From Ritual to Romance.*[12] Perhaps we should add that the espousal of this interpretation by T. S. Eliot in *The Waste Land* (1922) tended to foster its spread. There are few critics today who favor such an explanation although the theory has found entry into many reference books, and students who have not made a special study of the Grail material are sometimes surprised to learn that it is not the latest, current, Grail theory.

Miss Weston finds the explanation for the Grail legend in the Adonis cult, which, she hypothesizes, had persisted through the ages among occult sects. In the twelfth idyll of Theocritus the slain god is stretched on a bed with wailing women around him. No details are given. Adonis, Miss Weston claimed, is the maimed Fisher King of the Grail Castle. This King and the god Adonis have both been castrated, that is, wounded in the thighs. The wasting of the land around the Grail Castle is due, she claims, to the death of the Vegetation Spirit. The accomplishment of Perceval's Quest will restore Adonis to life and to health. The Grail is a symbol of the female organ, and the Lance of the male.

To most worshippers this resurrection would have been only a means of restoring fruitfulness: to the elect it would mean initiation into the mystery of the origins of physical life. The Grail at the lower level was just a food-producing vessel—but in the ultimate stage it no longer had material substance. Miss Weston claimed that "occultists" among her friends attested the similarities between their rites and this Grail interpretation. She thought that Gawain, not Perceval, was the Grail hero in the primitive un-Christianized version. It was at Glastonbury that all this was later associated with Christianity. Joseph of Arimathea was accepted there as the Apostle of Britain, and could easily have been connected with a relic of the Sacred Blood.

We have listed Miss Weston's theory before a similar one proposed by William A. Nitze because we believe that Nitze may have been inspired by the first volume of Miss Weston's book (see above), which appeared in 1906; also, Nitze did not persist for long in his Ritualist interpretation. In later years he inclined towards the Celtic theories, with some modifications of his own. He admitted a certain amount of the Christian explanation, particularly the association of the Grail Procession with the Byzantine Mass. For a full appreciation of Nitze's mature views on this, the reader should read his *Perceval and the Holy Grail: An Essay on the Romance of Chrétien de Troyes* (Berkeley and Los Angeles: University of California Press, 1949). Much of what he believed will also be found in W. A. Nitze and Harry F. Williams, *Arthurian Names in the Perceval of Chrétien de Troyes: Analysis and Commentary* (Berkeley and Los Angeles: University of California Press, 1955). Although not in agreement with much of what Nitze has written on the *Perceval*, the present writer feels that what Nitze had to say about the *Perlesvaus* (see below) shows another direction to which he could have turned. Nitze was a great scholar, and we wish to pay this tribute to him here.

Nitze, in 1909,[13] saw the Grail legend as a continuation of a vegetation cult, making his comparisons with the ancient Eleusinian Mysteries of the Greeks. The procession, then, was an initiation ceremony intended to admit the qualified individual into the preservation of the Vegetation Spirit. The Fisher King, he thought, was a figure from the Underworld—an intermediary between this Otherworld existence and our human life. He was associated with water. His lameness was evidence of his declining vigor and his land lay in waste because of enchantment. The initiate, Perceval, was destined to promote the success of the Grail service; otherwise, springs would dry up and the crops would wither.

The figure in the Inner room may have been the result of an error on Chrétien's part. He is not found in other twelfth and thirteenth century Grail stories. If his presence is not an error, he is meant to represent the life-god—perhaps Osiris or Adonis. The Grail vessel is the sacred box which, it is assumed, was part of the Eleusinian Mystery. This contained the sacred food which the initiate shared with the vegetation god. The Grail box, therefore, preserves from decay and also feeds. It causes true believers to be distinguished from the non-believers. Through the legend of the Holy Blood, as at Glastonbury, this box came to be identified with the cup of the Last Supper. The monks at Fécamp claimed to possess a relic of the Sacred Blood. The bleeding lance is a symbol of light, such as one finds in Celtic tales. Nitze admitted the possibility that there was a parallel to the Greek Eleusinian Mysteries among the Celts—and that this Grail procession could have come directly from the Celtic version. He compared Mannanan mac Lir, the Celtic god, with the Fisher King, and the lance with the one made by Gronw in the *Math Son of Mathonwy* (the third branch of the *Mabinogi*). This lance was intended for the treacherous slaying of Llew Llaw Gyffes.

X *Celtic Explanations*

This brings us to the Celtic interpretation of the Grail mysteries. The Celtic Theory has been held steadfastly by so many Arthurian scholars that it has had an almost official status for about fifty years. During much of this time the leading scholar among the *Celtisants* (as they are often called) was the late Professor Roger Sherman Loomis (1886–1965). Not all those who prefer the Celtic interpretation are in perfect agreement, and Loomis himself altered certain opinions from time to time, but a general statement of the *Celtisant* position can be made from Chapter XXI in Loomis' volume *Arthurian Literature in the Middle Ages*, to which we already have had frequent occasion to refer.

The *Celtisants* call attention to the fact that the details in Chrétien's *Conte dou Graal* and in the other Grail stories cannot be harmonized. They think, therefore, that there is no unified basic purpose in these legends: a medley of old Celtic themes with a nature myth as kernel that has been adapted somewhat ingeniously to the manners and ideas of medieval France.

The legend of Arthur, they say, first sprang up in Wales. The Fisher King was named Bron, and it can hardly be a coincidence that Bran the son of Llyr was also wounded in battle by a spear. This wounding, in the case of Bran as in the case of Chrétien's Fisher King, was followed by a "wasting" of Britain. They also point out that a Welsh List called the Thirteen Treasures of Britain included the Platter of Rhydderch, a platter supposedly identical in form and shape with the Grail vessel. On the Welsh platter any food that one desires will appear.[14] Loomis says that the Welsh platter belonged originally to Bran, and not to Rhydderch, who was an historical king of Strathclyde in the sixth century. The knight whom we call Perceval is a continuation of the Welsh Pryderi—who was a nephew of this Bran. Pryderi brought on the desolation of southwestern Wales by sitting on a perilous mound after a banquet (see the *Manawydan Fab Llyr*). Perceval, according to the *Didot Perceval*, brought on terrible enchantments by sitting on the Siege Perilous before a banquet.

It is agreed, says Loomis, that Wales absorbed a great deal of mythic and heroic material from Ireland during the Dark Ages. Therefore, much of the Grail romance is foreshadowed in the Irish sagas. There is great similarity between the visits to the Grail Castle and those scenes in the Irish sagas where a mortal visits the palace of a god or goddess.

Such a parallel appears in *The Prophetic Ecstasy of the Phantom* (*Baile in Scáil*), which was written before 1056. In it, Conn goes to the dwelling of a phantom horseman who turns out to be Lug. He finds there a crowned damsel on a crystal chair, and Lug himself on a throne. The damsel, Lug's wife, serves King Conn with vast quantities of meat. She serves ale in a golden cup. "To whom shall this be given?" she asks. Lug mentions the names of those who will rule at Tara. Then the phantom and his palace disappear, but the cup and the vessel remain with Conn. Loomis thinks that this damsel on the crystal seat is the Grail Bearer in Chrétien's poem. Since Lug's wife can assume a hideous appearance, Loomis and other *Celtisants* have proposed that the Hideous Damsel who comes to Arthur's court is this Grail bearer in disguise. The spear of Lug, which later was called the *Luin* of Celtchar (Celtchar acquired it), is described as dripping blood on one occasion—and in still another text it is associated with a cauldron of blood. Here Loomis definitely suggests that the Irish *Baile in Scáil*, in some way, supplied the "basic outline" for Chrétien's *Perceval* or *Conte dou Graal*.

Loomis says, in sum:

> . . . the origin of the Grail romances lies very clearly in the fund of Irish and Welsh stories exploited by the Breton conteurs, and we need no longer wonder at their diversity and irrationality. But there is still reason to wonder why those particular legends were so persistently given a Christian colouring. (*ibid.*, p. 284)

Loomis always insisted that the actual contact which Chrétien had with such Celtic sources was through Breton narrators—that is, through continental Celts. The men of letters who preceded and followed Chrétien were confused by it all, he said. They saw the expression *cors beneiz*—and they confused *cor* "horn (of plenty)" with *cors* from *Corpus Domini*. Even before Chrétien the Celtic platter was associated with Christian attributes, and not long after this the maimed Fisher King was linked with Joseph of Arimathea, who had been custodian of the Holy Body. The association of Joseph and the Conversion of Britain was exploited at Glastonbury.

M. Jean Marx, who knows his Celtic sagas very well, and is considerably influenced by A. C. L. Brown, W. A. Nitze, and many of the American *Celtisants,* agrees that the Arthurian material is "of pagan and profane origin," [15] and that, under influence from Glastonbury and then from Clairvaux, it took on a Christian color. The Treasures of the Irish Tuatha Dé Danann account for the Grail and the Lance. The Quest of Perceval is a summons from the Otherworld. The Sickness and suffering of the ruler of that region (the Fisher King) bring on a failure of fertility. The grail, or Cup of Plenty, provides the feast. The sovereignty of the earthly King is restored when the Grail hero has conquered the Marvelous Treasures.

XI *Oriental Explanations*

As might be expected, there have been efforts to interpret the meaning of Chrétien's Grail by reference to Oriental religions. Pierre Ponsoye says:

Among all the problems which are posed [by the fact that the teaching of the Grail is an esoteric grandmastership] the one which has attracted the least attention of Romance scholars is the Islamic influence which is to be observed on at least one of the chief and primitive branches of the Cycle: the *Parzival* of Wolfram von Eschenbach . . . It is clear that Christianity and Islam in the Middle Ages were not directly in conflict. This spiritual conjuction is only the normal manifestation, although hidden, of the Mystery of Unity which unites metaphysically and in eschatology all the authentic revelations, and especially Judaism, Christianity, and Islam, common heirs of the great traditions of Abraham.[16]

Arthur U. Pope, in his "Persia and the Holy Grail," [17] finds parallels to the Grail in the legends of Persia. In *La lumiére du Graal,*[18] René Nelli suggests that the Grail legend is a tissue of ancient myths. "The Grail is no longer in the West" (p.

315). The Templars and the Albigensians, he says, may have had much to do with the propagation of the basic ideas behind it all.

In recent years, researchers who have not been convinced of the orthodox Christian origin of the Grail material have been turning to unorthodox Christianity. Foremost among these was the late Leonardo Olschki. Not long before his death he published in Italian a monograph on the subject.[19] This has now been translated by J. A. Scott and published under the title *The Grail Castle and Its Mysteries,*[20] along with a very encouraging foreword by Eugene Vinaver, who says that this treatment is "a thorough exposition of a theory which had never before been put forward with such an abundance of supporting evidence" (pp. viii ff.).

Olschki puts special emphasis on these lines in Chrétien's *Perceval*: "Jesus Christ the holy prophet to whom the Jews did great shame" (vss. 581–582). This, he concludes, is outright Gnosticism and is contrary to orthodox Christianity. (This is not quite clear to some of us, for it is orthodox Christian belief that Christ was Prophet, Priest, and King. See, for example, Luke 21:11, "This is Jesus the prophet from Nazareth of Galilee.") Olschki states that Perceval had no concept of the Divine Essence and that he did not practice any Christian worship. (But, of course, he *did* receive the Sacraments from the hermit.)

Olschki also believes that the religious phraseology in the *Perceval* is scant and merely conventional. (Perhaps so, but it is never unorthodox. It should be remembered that Perceval genuflects when he enters the hermit's chapel [vss. 6348–49], and that he participates in the Adoration of the Cross which follows after the Mass on Good Friday [vss. 6495–96].) Olschki attributes Gnostic meaning to the fact that the young Perceval (without a name as yet) thinks the knights whom he meets are devils— but asserts that they are angels when the light shines on their armor, and even asks one of them if he is God Himself (vss. 144 ff.). (To us it does not seem, as it does to Olschki, that the young man in this passage was viewing God as light— which is a Gnostic and Manichaean belief.)

Finally, Olschki states that Perceval's sin in deserting his mother was done without Free Will. (But the boy says precisely: "Give me something to eat. I don't know what you are telling me—but

I shall *willingly* go to the king who makes the knights. I shall go, whoever may be bothered by it." These words certainly indicate that Perceval was obeying Free Will and therefore was not unorthodox in this respect. As Perceval leaves the castle of Gornemant the latter bids him (vss. 1663–64) frequent the Church and pray to God the Creator of all things that He may have pity on his soul and keep him a faithful Christian. The youth replies, "My mother spoke to me just as you are doing. . . ." Obviously, to judge from these lines, the young Perceval has been taught the Creed and other prayers, which he uses when he drops on his knees before the knights (vss. 155–58). He has had orthodox instruction. Of his own Free Will he neglects what he has been taught. There is no Gnostic heresy here.)

Let me remind our readers that the Gnostics taught that "knowledge," not faith, good works, or ritual gave salvation. They rejected completely the Old Testament. They were influenced strongly by Neo-Platonism and by Manichaeism. Through worship of Wisdom one could rise from the material world and go to the Savior, who dwelt in the Plerome (world above) with Wisdom and reflected Truth, and among the other beings. Christians, through their faith in Jesus Christ, could attain only lesser salvation. In his foreword, Professor Vinaver says: "Chrétien de Troyes' *Conte de Graal* is to be interpreted as a drama between heresy and faith, damnation and redemption" (p. viii).

Henry and Renée Kahane have a theory which may have been influenced somewhat by Leonardo Olschki, whose theory we have just outlined.[21] The Kahanes point out that Chrétien and Wolfram von Eschenbach both had written sources; but Wolfram claimed that his account (based on Kyot) was superior to that narrated by Chrétien. Kyot then would have had a right to be angry with Chrétien.

The Kahanes believe that Chrétien's source was Apuleius' *Metamorphoses,* or *Golden Ass,* Books. I–XI. Wolfram, however, would have used the *Corpus hermeticum,* Treatise IV, which is called *The Krater.* For Chrétien, the Isis material in Apuleius was entirely new, so he wove it into his religious plot. But Wolfram took the Hermetic doctrine of *his* predecessor quite seriously, and therefore scorned Chrétien's lack of true understanding.

We will give a quote from the section in Book XI of the *Metamorphoses* of Apuleius where the "strange and grotesque masquerade," the anteludia of the real Isis procession, occurs. The Kahanes think that this contains the essence of Chrétien's Grail symbols.

Behold, then more and more appeared the beginnings of the pomps and processions, everyone attired in regal manner, according to his proper habit. One was girded about the middle like a man of arms; another bare a spear, and had a cloak caught up and high shoes as a hunter; another was attired in a robe of silk, and socks of gold, with fine ornament, having long hair added and fixed upon his head, and walked delicately in form of a woman; there was another which wore a leg harness and bore a target, an helmet, and a sword, like unto a gladiator, as one might believe; after him marched one attired in purple, with the rods borne by vergers before him, like a magistrate; after him followed one with a mantle, a staff, a pair of pantofles, and with a beard as long as any goat's, signfying a philosopher; after him went one with reeds and lime, betokening him a fowler, and another with hooks, declaring a fisher. I saw there a meek and tame bear, which in matron habit was carried on a stool; an ape with a bonnet of woven stuff on his head, and covered with saffron lawn, resembling the Phrygian shepherd Ganymede, and bearing a cup of gold in his hand; an ass had wings glued to his back and went after an old man, whereby you would judge the one to be Pegasus and the other Bellerophon, and at both would you laugh well.[22]

The Kahanes make parallels between this and Chrétien's Grail procession. The fisherman is the Fisher King. The weak old man is equated with the old man in the Inner room who had been fed by the Grail for fifteen years. The bear is on a stool, which was represented by Chrétien as the Fisher King's bed. The fashionable "woman" (who is really a male prostitute) is the source for the Grail maiden. The hunter's spear might be the lance; the gladiator has a *ferrum*, or sword. Above all, the golden cup carried by Ganymede suggests the Grail vessel.

This tale of the conversion of Lucius (the former ass) to the Isis religion may well be reflected, the Kahanes say, in the conversion of Perceval. We will not try to argue against this here. The reader should bear in mind, however, that the emphasis is very different between Apuleius and Chrétien, and that much of the Isis *preludia* has to be omitted in a comparison with the Grail procession.

Very recently, Silvestro Fiore joined those who wish to see a vegetation myth in the Grail legend—but he too assumes that this came from the cult of Isis and Osiris in Egypt.[23] Dr. Fiore agrees that Jessie L. Weston was the first to orientate Grail research in this direction. According to Egyptian lore, he says, Horus, the posthumous son of Osiris, seeks to rouse Osiris from the prostration of death. He opens Osiris' mouth with a lance, and embraces him. A cup or box containing the liquid of vivification plays an important part. Dr. Fiore expects shortly to establish a relationship between Celtic folklore and ancient Oriental myths. He holds that the phallic nature of the Grail was obliterated in the West by a new interpretation of the "sacred relic" as a ciborium or chalice. We find one of Dr. Fiore's assertions unclear:

> When since the ninth century, during the reign of Charles the Bald, numerous Scotch and Irish refugees crossed the Channel to avoid the Viking invasions, the *matière de Bretagne* penetrated gradually into the repertoire of French story tellers, among whom were the wandering clerks so well known by reason of their Graeco-Oriental legends.

There are some correspondences in Fiore's material with what has been proposed by the Kahanes and Olschki. These theories of Gnostic and Egyptian Ritual origin have been very recently presented, and we are aware that the brief sketches we have given are insufficient. Our readers should do these theories more justice by consulting the scholarly works in which they have been presented.

XII *Chrétien and the* Peredur

It is interesting that no one today is disposed to argue vigorously that Chrétien in his *Conte dou Graal* was intending to repeat the solution given in the Welsh *Peredur the Son of Evrawc,* where the hoary-headed man of the Grail Castle is the protagonist's mother's brother (and the brother of the man who instructed him). In the Welsh work, two youths enter, one bearing a great spear from the point of which three streams of blood flow onto the ground. Two maidens carry a platter on which is a man's bloody head. Peredur asks no question. Many adventures later a black maiden, quite hideous, comes to Arthur's court and upbraids Peredur for not having asked questions at the court of the Lame King, for he could thereby have restored the King to health and wealth. Peredur again seeks the castle. When he finds it, a yellow-haired boy, his cousin, says that, he was the black maiden, and that he was also the youth who held the bleeding lance. The head belonged to Peredur's cousin, slain by the witches of Gloucester who also had maimed the King. Arthur is summoned to attack the witches. Only Peredur is able to kill one of them. The rest try to flee, but Peredur and his followers kill them all. Peredur had been destined to avenge his uncle and thus free him from enchantments.

Although many plot details are similar in this Welsh *Peredur* and in Chrétien's poem, the multiple magic episodes and primitive quest themes in the Welsh version make it probable that they do not expound the same basic theme. But what is the relationship of these two? The *Conte dou Graal* and the *Peredur* cannot be far apart in date. It is usual to state that the Welsh storyteller knew Chrétien's romance, but there is always the possibility that both were familiar with a work by the same predecessor.

This, of course, is a haunting problem. Are the details of Chrétien's story original with him, or did that "book" which, he says, came to him from Count Philip of Flanders, contain material on the Grail, the Bleeding Lance, and the Quest? We will answer this in the negative, preferring to believe that the Welsh narrator had learned the elements of Chrétien's unfinished romance and, doubtless from memory, had spun a yarn of his own.

This whole matter has been thoroughly discussed by scholars. I. L. Foster gives a fine summary of the arguments on all sides.[24] He himself believes that Chrétien used another French romance (now lost) as a source, and that this same source was known to the author of the *Peredur*. He suggests that Chrétien also followed predecessors in the base of the *Erec* and the *Yvain*. It would be rather remarkable if all three of these predecessors had disappeared without any trace—except those that can be conjectured in Chrétien's work and in Welsh adaptations.

It is a logical conclusion from the variety of the theories that we have been outlining that, in the opinion of many medievalists, the *meaning* or *sens* of the symbolism employed by Chrétien in his *Perceval* has not been satisfactorily interpreted. The problem still remains to be explored. Many of the textbooks used by graduate students tend to present the theories of Celtic origin as though they were universally accepted; but such views should be received with caution. Scholars inclined toward Celtic explanations have not distinguished sufficiently between possible folk sources for details of the Grail story, and the vastly more important problem: *Why* was the Grail story composed? If Chrétien had a purpose in composing his romance, if his work contains a "message," we should concentrate on exposing this to the best of our ability before we content ourselves with the mere listing of folk motifs. The following chapter is an approach toward a possible understanding of Chrétien's "message."

CHAPTER 10

The Judeo-Christian Theory of the Grail

Most of those who have written on the origins of the Grail legend have been willing to admit that Christian interpretation of certain details crept into the material as it was treated by Chrétien. They insist, however, that the main figures of the narrative action, and, in particular, the objects carried in the Grail procession, had their roots in pagan mysteries or in details of non-Christian mythology. They do *not* admit that there was any plan for a didactic message, through Christian symbolism, when this Christianizing took place. The small amount of Christianization could be owed to the Abbey of Glastonbury, they say, or perhaps to the Benedictine Abbey of Fécamp in Normandy, where there was preserved a legend of the Holy Blood. If Chrétien's Grail had any didactic purpose, it would be as an "instruction book" for a perfect knight, perhaps intended to guide young Philip Augustus, who assumed the kingship of France around the first of November in 1179. He was then fourteen years old.

Some of the proponents of the Christian origin of the Grail legend, and definitely those who hold the Judeo-Christian theory, believe that, beginning with Chrétien at least, the legend was intended to convey an allegory of Christian teaching. Even where Chrétien made use of episodes from Celtic and other non-Christian sources, these were purposefully woven into the whole. Our use of the word allegory is disputed by some of those who do not agree. We will define this with dictionary in hand: an allegory is a story in which a spiritual or poetic meaning is conveyed by symbols. It may seem to many that there is not a great deal keeping Grail critics apart. We all accept the influence of non-Christian legends and other non-Christian source materials, and both sides agree that there was an eventual Christianization. The disagreement centers on the amount of intended symbolism found in the poem, and the suggested "message."

Our procedure in this last chapter will be, first, to suggest the *probability* that there was an allegorical plan in the basic episodes of the *Conte dou Graal.* We will then propose that the Continuators, and the writers of the prose Grail Romances, had some understanding of Chrétien's plan. More difficult to establish is our belief that the conversion of the Jews to Christianity, particularly in Champagne, was a burning Quest among theologians, and amateur theologians (like Chrétien?), during the last quarter of the twelfth century—provoked in part by the intolerance generated by preparations for another Crusade, even earlier than the fall of Jerusalem in 1187 after the Battle of Hittin; and in part by growing resentment on the part of many Christians in those areas where Jewish prosperity and freedom were very marked under the reigns of Louis VII and Henry II of England. Violent persecution was in the making, and its manifestation only waited for the disappearance of the old kings, who were "tolerant" for different reasons. Peaceful and merciful conversion was the hope of the better thinkers, and there was fresh study of such ideas long expressed in the existing conversion literature, particularly in the Song of Songs, (which was so interpreted) and in the Epistle to the Hebrews. St. Bernard preached eighty-six sermons on the Song of Songs, mostly on the first two chapters which treat of sensual love that could become divine. Helinandus of Froidmont wrote a major commentary on it; and there were many others.

I   *Christian Allegory*

It is a major task to convince our medievalist colleagues that Christian allegory, rather than non-Christian elements, was behind the "quest themes" of twelfth-century literature. Some of us have a feeling that the soul's quest for special Grace was what Chrétien and a few other poets were contemplating. Mrs. Sargent may have had something of this idea of "regeneration" in mind (see the reference to her in our Chapter I), but she did not attach any thought of religious conversion to her thesis.

Certain patterns have convinced us that Christian allegory is the prime basis of the principal episodes of Chrétien's Grail poem. In the *Conte dou Graal* there are frequent mentions of the Isles as a land where graceless or unredeemed people dwell. Perceval's parents came from there, and Perceval's mother says to him: "There was no knight of so great worth, so feared, so respected, dear son, as was your father in all the Illes de Mer . . . I too am born of knights, of the best of that country; in the Illes de Mer there was no family better than mine . . ." (vss. 416–26). A wicked giant Rithon or Rion is sometimes mentioned as being king of these people (vss. 851–52).[1]

We assume that one approached the Isles, a sort of Never-Never Land, by crossing the Perilous Ford into Galloway, the land of the Picts and the Scots. Orgueilleus del Passage a Estroite Voie points out the border to Gawain: "No knight can return from there who might go there or see some of it, for that is the border [*bosne*] of Galloway, which no knight can cross if he wishes to return" (vss. 6598–4). The lady love of this Orgueilleus del Passage is Orgueilleuse de Logres; she is a distraught woman. The bad seneschal of Engygneron, who is besieging Blanchefleur in Belrepaire, is Clamadeus des Illes (vs. 2115). The lady whom the young Perceval kissed, and whose ring he took in innocence, is maltreated by her knight because of this misadventure of the kiss and the ring. The cruel knight is Orgueilleus de la Lande, who wants nothing so much as battle and fighting (vss. 3817–19). The hideous damsel on the yellow mule must return immediately to the Chastel Orgueilleus: "in the Castle there are 566 brave knights . . . each has his lady beside him . . . no one who goes there fails to find jousting and battle" (vss. 4691–4700).

The Isles, and these individuals with the name Orgueilleus ("proudful") may result from some Celtic tradition (Orgueilleus de la Lande was first cited as a character by Chrétien in his *Erec*), but for us it is clear that there is a firmly embedded

allegory here. These people must be brought to the "light"—
and the young man who will learn that his name is Perceval
had been a child of the people of the Isles. He too must be
converted.

The name Perceval must have allegorical meaning at the point
when it is introduced into the Grail poem (it too occurred previously in the *Erec* and the *Lancelot*). The young woman with
the headless knight in her lap asks the hero of the Grail:

"What is your name, my friend?" And he who had not known
his name began to guess; he said that he was called Perceval le
Gallois. He did not know whether he spoke the truth or not; but he
spoke the truth and did not realize it. When the girl heard him
she got to her feet and spoke as in anger. "Your name is changed,
my dear sir." (vss. 3572–87)

Although those who argue for non-Christian origins are more
concerned with Chrétien's sources than they are with the intent
that Chrétien had in mind when he composed the *Conte dou
Graal,* they probably would be willing to admit that the Being
in the Inner room, the father of the Fisher King, must be identified in connection with Christian allegory. He eats no fasting
food (fish) but is served "with a single host which one carries
to him in that Grail; it sustains and comforts him, so holy
a thing is the Grail; he is spiritual and needs for his existence
nothing except the host which comes in the Grail" (vss. 6422–
28). It has been suggested that *oiste* could mean "oyster" rather
than Host, and proposed by others that the passage has no
meaning at all; but that kind of interpretation can hardly be
maintained.

In the same way, the verbal description of the Grail vessel
is so "glowing" that it could hardly have been applied by a
Christian cleric, in a Christian milieu, to anything but a sacred
vessel: "The Grail which went before was of fine pure gold;
on the Grail there were precious stones of many kinds, of the
richest and the most expensive which exist on sea or on land;
those of the Grail, without a doubt, surpass all other stones"
(vss. 3232–39).

It would be pointless to expatiate further *here* on what we
consider actual signs of Christian allegory. For further discussion

the reader can consult our book (with Sister M. Amelia Klenke, O.P., as co-author) which gives more detailed suggestions.[2] We quote further a statement by Martin de Riquer:[3]

Even if one supposes that by some route or other an ancient legend from a Celtic land reaches Chrétien de Troyes, it is nonetheless quite sure that *Li Contes del Graal* is a romance that is essentially Christian in which there come into play Christian elements that can be identified perfectly—which harmonize extremely well with the mentality, culture, and beliefs of France at the close of the twelfth century when this romance was born. As an educative work *Li Contes del Graal*, thanks to a young protagonist, unspoiled, half savage, develops a complete theory of the formation in knighthood, in military knowledge, in spiritual courtesy, in religion of this young man. Perceval was destined, beyond any doubt, to offer to society of his day the model of the perfect knight who is at the same time a perfect Christian. This is an ideal which St. Bernard presented to the Knights Templar in his treatise *De Laude novae militiae*. (1128–36)

The late Mario Roques, who, over many years, was a veritable Socrates for scholars in Old French literature, finally agreed that the Grail was a chalice (probably that of the Last Supper), that the beautiful Damsel carrying this was Ecclesia, that the *tailleor* was probably the plate used by Christ at the breaking of the bread at the Last Supper, that the Bleeding Lance was the Lance of the Passion, and that the bearer of the Lance was Longinus.[4]

II *Judeo-Christian Theory*

Sister Amelia Klenke, O.P., and I have been more specific in outlining the Christian parable which we see in the *Perceval*. We think that Chrétien was depicting the story of a young man, destined for the greatest of things, who did not yet know his destiny—to relieve the people who were led by the Fisher King. He progressed somewhat slowly. He lost his complete innocence and came to Arthur's court, which, we believe, represented the civilized community of England, as opposed to the Land of the Isles (north of the Solway Firth?).

After his first reception in Arthur's court, the young man learned how to be a knight (but still a Grace-less knight) from Gornemant; then he met Blanchefleur in her unhappy but Godly city. (We reject the idea that he spent a night in sin with her.[5] Chrétien mentions three times that he did not do anything of the kind. Here are the passages in question: "All the comfort and pleasure that one can provide in a bed did the knight have that night—except pleasure with a girl (if he wished) or with a lady (if he might do so). He knew nothing of love and he went to sleep in good time" [vss. 1937–43]; the girl when she came to him remarked: "Although I am unclothed I have not thought of any folly, evil, or low behavior" [vss. 1986–88]; again she says: "that she did not come to weep over his face except that she might make him understand and encourage him to undertake her battle" [vss. 2040–46]. Although she lay beside him, "they slept until daybreak" [vss. 2069]. Perceval's mother had counseled him not to be too friendly with women: "If a damsel grants you a kiss, I forbid you anything further" [vss. 547–48].)

The young man, who still does not know his name, then has the adventure of the Grail Castle. This is the central theme of the allegory and for this we will give our interpretation a little further on, after we have said something about the Ecclesia-Sinagoga motif. Afterwards, Perceval learns his name, and we feel sure he divined the true meaning of this name. He returns to Arthur's court.

A hideous damsel, mounted on a yellow mule—a bad omen—arrives at the court. She urges everyone present to seek the Bleeding Lance. She has come from the Chastel Orgueilleus. Just as we observed in the *Lancelot,* there is now a double quest shared by Perceval and Gawain. Gawain is a fine but worldly knight. Perceval is destined to receive Grace. We believe that Chrétien intended a constant parallel between the two men in these subsequent adventures. Gawain is proclaimed to be a wonderful knight by a little maid—the same has happened to Perceval. Gawain is besought carnally by the sister of the king of Escavalon; Perceval had been sought in spiritual relation by Blanchefleur. Gawain is badly treated by a young lady who has a knight's head in her lap; Perceval is taunted by a lady who has a headless knight in her lap.

We hear no more of Perceval and his quest after he receives Grace following his confession and Absolution from the holy hermit, his relative. But Gawain passes into the land of the strange people outside the bounds of Logres, Arthur's kingdom. There he encounters his sister, his mother Anna, and his grandmother Ygerne (the mother of Arthur). He becomes lord of their castle. He leaves this castle for charitable reasons, despite having been forbidden to do so. He sends to Arthur at Orcanie, desiring his presence for a crucial duel. At this point Chrétien laid down his pen—forever. If he had continued, we feel that Perceval would have gone on to the Grail Castle and enjoyed a spiritual victory paralleling in some form Gawain's physical triumphs. We shall never know. But the ultimate outcome for Perceval should have been the bringing of Grace and Conversion to those in the Grail Castle—which was, we believe, the ultimate goal being suggested by Chrétien.

When Sister Amelia and I began our investigations of Chrétien's great poem, we took the position that the Grail romances which followed directly after Chrétien's should not be included in our consideration. We were concerned only with the circumstances which incited Chrétien to write as he did. This was a mistake. The works of Robert of Boron: the *Joseph of Arimathea*, the *Merlin*, and the Didot *Perceval* (if this was composed by Robert), as well as the anonymous *Perlesvaus* in prose (which Nitze dated between 1191 and 1212), and the anonymous *Queste del Saint Graal* (early thirteenth century) may well have preserved much of the basic "message" that was intended by Chrétien. Those who oppose this claim say that when these were written the process of Christianizing the Grail legend had gone beyond Chrétien, and that additional mysteries and a *new* spirit had already penetrated the world of chivalry.[6]

Robert of Boron in his *Joseph of Arimathea* mentions (vss. 932–36) a great book which contains the secret of the Grail; but later states explicitly that no one but himself had ever written about this subject matter (Epilogue). Apparently Robert did not feel that he had completed his narrative. He intended to handle later on the facts pertaining to his characters Alain, Moyses, and Bron (or Hebron) (see his vss. 3501–7); in the meanwhile, he passed on to the story of Merlin. It is reasonable to assume that Robert was piecing together various materials that he did not fully understand: biblical and apocryphal themes, and possibly some information from Glastonbury. He must certainly have known Chrétien's *Conte dou Graal,* but perhaps only imperfectly.

We can assume from this that some accounts of the history and powers of the Grail, the Vessel of the Last Supper, existed for a time prior to Chrétien and Robert of Boron. *There is no reason for believing that such a lost source, or sources, was in narrative romance form.* The Didot *Perceval* (in prose), which is certainly later than Chrétien's work, continues on with this. It gives a solution to the Grail problem which surely was not Chrétien's. In it Perceval (the son of Alain) returns to the Grail Castle where he asks the question. Immediately the Fisher King is healed and, at the command of the Holy Ghost, teaches the secrets of the Grail to Perceval and leaves the Vessel with him. The Fisher King then dies on the third day.[7] The Didot *Perceval* may be dated 1202; the *Joseph of Arimathea,* about 1200.

The *Perlesvaus* is obviously associated with Eucharistic tradition. In it "The New Law or Testament is everywhere placed in opposition to the Old Law, which includes not only the Jews but the heathen in general . . . the Damsels of the Cart arrive and urge him [Perceval] to destroy the Old Law by delivering the Grail castle from the King of Castle Mortal." This quotation is taken from the late W. A. Nitze's treatment of the *Perlesvaus.*[8] Another quotation: "In *Perlesvaus* Arthur and his knights establish the New Law [New Testament] at the point of the sword. The importance of the Sinagoga-Ecclesia contrast is thus not as new as we once suggested. It is admittedly in Robert de Boron and the *Perlesvaus.*"

In view of such remarks as these by Nitze and others, it is strange that so many of those concerned with the story of the Grail in Chrétien should have been repulsed and shocked by our Judeo-Christian explanation.

Chrétien began his *Conte dou Graal* with the statement that one must sow his seed on good ground if it is to grow and flourish. The romance was composed, he says, for Philip of Alsace, count of Flanders, whom the poet lauds as being superior to the great Alexander. Alexander brought together in himself all vices and ills; but the count abhors evil and loves Justice and the Church. The count gives most generously, and never ostentatiously. He is inspired by Charity which, as St. Paul has said, is God Himself, whereas Alexander cared not a whit for Charity. Chrétien was commanded by the count of Flanders to rhyme the finest tale which has ever been told at a royal court, and the source for this, a book, has been given him by the count (vss. 1–68).

Philip of Flanders was a frequent visitor to the court at Troyes and became a confidant of the Countess Marie de Champagne after the death of her husband in 1181. Count Philip himself died ten years later in the Holy Land. A great fire at Troyes in 1188 spread to the area of the count's palace and probably destroyed documents which would have helped us in piecing together some of the details of the circumstances preceding the composition of Chrétien's *Conte dou Graal*.

A great mystery is the identity of the "book" which Chrétien claims was given him by his new patron, Count Philip. It is customary to deny that the book existed, but there is no proof either way. It can be assumed that Chrétien was associated with Philip of Flanders after the death of Henry of Troyes in 1181. It is not at all likely that Chrétien moved from the Troyes area. It was not necessary. Philip was, after all, peripatetic. Need we remind the reader once again that the theme suggested from the "source" book was the Quest of the Bleeding Lance, and of the Grail? The hideous damsel makes this clear in the *Conte dou Graal*:

Ha! Perceval, Fortune is bald behind and with much hair in front. May he be accursed who greets you, or who may wish you well. When you met Fortune you did not receive her. You entered into the dwelling of the Fisher King and saw the Bleeding Lance. It was so much trouble for you to open your mouth and speak that you could not ask why that drop of Blood falls from the point of the Lance; nor about the Grail which you saw did you ask anything, nor did you inquire what good man was served from it. [This is the Being in the Inner room] . . . And do you know what will happen because of this King who will not hold his land? Ladies will lose their husbands, lands will be destroyed, girls will be without help, will become orphans. Many knights will die because of it; all these evils will be because of you. (vss. 4646–83)

The Quest of the Lance and the Grail would be in the interest of Charity, and this will be the finest tale which has ever been told in royal court. The purpose of this *Conte dou Graal* was to bring about a great Good, figuratively speaking. This was no small matter. Later, one of the vassals of the king of Escavalon proposes that Gawain be released for a year provided he swears to seek out "the Lance of which the point weeps; and it is written that some day all the kingdom of Logres, which used to belong to the Giants [*Ogres*] will be destroyed because of that Lance. . . ." We assume that the Giants were the subjects of Rion or Rithon, the king of the Isles who used to own the land of Logres—who will get it back someday by force unless the Quest is accomplished.[9] The Giants we consider the evil folk, the non-Christian world. Chrétien's, and Philip of Flanders', thesis, may have been that such a conquest, going the other way, could be achieved by Charity rather than by force.

We are suggesting that Chrétien, who may well have been in retirement from his work as a court poet during the 1175–85 period, was in the 1180's urged to do a vaster, more important romance by Count Philip of Flanders. This romance, we suggest, had something to do with a great social Good. Chrétien says in detail:

Charity does not boast of her good works; instead she conceals so that no one will know her except God, and God can be called both God and Charity. God is Charity, and he who lives by her, as St. Paul has said (and I have read this) lives in God and God in him. (vss. 43–50)

In his Sermon No. LXXIX, St. Bernard spoke of the need for showing Charity to the Jews, of whom there was a very large population in Champagne:

The great Charity of the Church, which does not wish to withhold its delights from its rival Sinagoga . . . Indeed, what can be more charitable than when someone is ready to communicate to an enemy that which his soul loves. This is marvelous that Salvation comes from the Jews . . . Our Saviour has returned to the place from whence He came so that those who are left of Israel may be saved. The branches are not ungrateful to the root nor the sons to the mother . . . The Church has Salvation in its keeping until all people may come to it. Thus all of Israel can be saved . . .[10]

A striking characteristic of the Troyes area in the mid-period of the twelfth century was the growth and activity of the great Jewish community there. This explains, to be sure, why the region was famous for its fairs and its commerce—not to mention its banking. The Jews were greatly concerned with commerce. There were many, many conversions from Judaism to Christianity; but in times of stress such conversions were often brought about by force.

Troyes was an important center for a dialectic of the Conversion of the Jews. The Knights Templar received their statutes in Troyes in 1128. The Premonstratensian Canons were first established in the Troyes district, and conversion of the Jews was one of their chief concerns. Moreover, the big Forêt de l'Orient between the Seine and the Aube rivers, to the east of Troyes and west of Bar-sur-Aube, was a favorite retreat for holy hermits. Also, the Conversion of Sinagoga to Ecclesia was a favorite theme in art at this time. As Sister Amelia has shown, there were representations of this at Châlons and Saint-Denis, and in many of the great cathedrals. Perhaps the finest is at Strasbourg. In these thirteenth century carvings, Sinagoga is a lady with a lance, often broken, and she is sometimes blindfolded. Ecclesia, of course, is a lovely lady in glory, holding a chalice. I have seen a mural painting of this, dating from the twelfth century, on the wall of a church in the Holy Land, at the site which the Crusaders identified with Emmaus.

III Grail Procession

Now we come to the Grail Procession. This must represent a procession of the Old Law (Sinagoga) which will be transmuted into the Ecclesia procession of the New Law. Under the Old Law, Sinagoga is herself the bearer of the Vessel. The vessel contains the sacred manna; the *tailleor* is the Tablet of the Law; and the lance is the Rod of Aaron. These, of course, are the talismans of the Holy of Holies of the Temple.[11] The Grail Hall is to be identified with the Temple, and the inner room with the Holy of Holies. The Fisher King, with his purple fringed garments, we think of as Jacob, the great High Priest. The Being in the Inner room we now identify as David, the first king of Jerusalem.

In the New Testament phase, the Being in the Inner room remained the same, for Christ is figuratively designated as the Son of David. When the question is asked, and the Old becomes the New, the Lady will be the figure of Ecclesia, bearing the Chalice of the Last Supper. The Bleeding Lance will be carried by Longinus; the *tailleor* will be the paten. The light bearers are first the two Cherubim of the Holy of Holies, and then become Angels of the New Law. Sinagoga is always represented with a lance, as we have recalled above. Perceval's great deed would have been to convert the Old Law into the New, thus bringing blessing to the land, to Christ (the King), and to men, women, orphans, and all.

In case one doubts the presence of Longinus we add this from the *Golden Legend* of Jacobus de Voragine:

> Longinus was the centurion who was assigned by Pilate to stand guard with his soldiers at the crucifixion of the Lord, and who pierced His side with a lance. He was converted to the Christian Faith when he saw the signs which followed upon the death of Jesus, namely the darkening of the sun and the quaking of the earth . . . He then quit the military life, receiving instruction from the Apostles and for twenty-eight years led the life of a monk at Caesarea of Cappadocia working many conversions by his word and his example.[12]

There can be little doubt of one thing, that responsible Christian thinkers and leaders, in the second half of the twelfth century, were concerned with a need for absorbing the Jews into the general Christian community. Such Conversion could be accomplished in one of two ways: by physical force or by charitable persuasion. Unhappily, they eventually *did* resort to force, even in Flanders.

IV   *Song of Songs*

Sister Amelia is convinced that all allegory of the Triumphant Church or Ecclesia in Chrétien appears in terms derived from the Song of Songs. This is why Ecclesia appears more as a lovely bride than as a solemn, crowned figure. The Commentary in the new Jerusalem Bible says:

The Jewish rabbis understood [the Song of Songs] allegorically: the relationship of the lower and beloved is that between God and Israel, the traditional prophetic marriage metaphor dating from Hosea. The writers of the early Church, with the exception of Theodore of Mopsuestia, adopted the same explanation, though with them the allegory becomes one of Christ and his Church [Ecclesia]. This allegorical interpretation is accepted, under various forms, by the great majority of Catholic commentators today. Some are content with the general theme, the elaboration being purely literary, of God the bridegroom of Israel. Others see in the sequence of the Song of Songs the story of Israel's changing seasons, of Conversion, Hope, Disillusionment.[13]

This statement almost parallels the idea of the transmutation of Sinagoga into Ecclesia.

V *The Word "Grail"*

For a definition of the term Grail as it was understood by Helinandus of Froidmont (born about 1150), we will quote a passage in full from his *Chronicon*. Often only a single phrase from this passage is quoted; this single phrase gives a distorted definition when taken by itself:

At that time in Brittany a marvelous vision was shown to a certain hermit by an angel, concerning the decurion St. Joseph who removed the Body of Our Lord from the Cross—also of a deep vessel [*catinus*] in which the Lord supped with His Disciples. From this a story was composed by the hermit which is called *De Gradalibus.* A *Gradalis* or *Gradale* is translated into French as *a broad eating dish,* somewhat deep, *in which very rich viands are customarily placed* in order, one portion after another, in varied arrangements. It is called in the vernacular, a *graalz,* because it is pleasant [*grata*] and acceptable for one eating this food; it contains, while being of silver or some other precious material, a multiplicity of precious festive foods.[14]

The etymology is, of course, fanciful, as we should expect from someone writing around 1200. Suffice it to say that for Helinandus, a grail is a rich vessel—somewhat deep and wide—which is used to display or contain ornamental food. There is no association with a "flat platter," as some scholars have insisted, while using this very text—and omitting most of its meaningful description.[15]

Froidmont (Aisne) is about eight miles north of Laon. We are concerned with what Helinandus could have meant by this description of a grail as a silver dish for containing, or displaying, festival foods—which we understand from him was an expensive *escuele* used for ritual purposes. Interestingly, such a dish is in regular use today. At the Passover service, in many Jewish homes, just such a bowl, a Seder plate, is used as a container for symbolic foods in celebration of the flight from Egypt. Perhaps Helinandus knew that the world Grail was used for such a symbolic dish among the Jews of his time. If the Seder plate could be associated with the vessel used by Christ at the Last Supper, this would be additional evidence for the Judeo-Christian theory.

Sister Amelia Klenke calls attention to the fact that in the Dominican Rite (following an early rite of Toulouse), the wine and water are poured into the chalice at the time the Gradual is sung. She suggests that the Latin word *gradualis* may be the source for the Old French word *graal*. She calls attention also to the fact that the chalice was not completely fixed in shape by the twelfth century; but that the beautiful chalice made for Abbot Suger, which is now in the Mellon Art Gallery in Washington, may well have been the actual cup which Chrétien had in mind. Chrétien describes just such a cup when he says:

> The Grail, which went before, was of fine refined gold; there were precious stones on the Grail of many kinds, of the richest and dearest that are on land or sea—those of the Grail surpassed all other stones without a doubt. (*Perceval*, vss. 3232–39)

The character of Perceval may have been modeled upon that of St. Paul. Chrétien states in his Prologue that he had been reading St. Paul. St. Paul was a great convert and the patron of medieval knights. When Perceval girds on the sword in the Grail Castle, there may have been an association in Chrétien's mind with Psalms 45:3–4: "Here, strap your sword at your side, in majesty and splendor; on, ride on, in the cause of truth, religion and virtue."

We believe that the symbol of the Grail Hall and of the Grail Procession was intended, on the recommendation of Philip of Flanders, to propagandize the concept of a Conversion of the Jews to Christianity through Charity and non-violent means. As we have stated above, this theme of the Conversion of the Synagogue into the Church was prevalent in contemporary art representations, and it had its scriptural authority in the Epistle to the Hebrews and the Song of Songs. The Grail is the Chalice of the Last Supper; the *oiste* or Host, carried in the Grail to the spiritual Being, was the Eucharist. The Inner room into which the Procession passed was the Jewish Holy of Holies. The man who carried the Bleeding Lance at the head of the Procession was representative of Longinus (who was considered the first convert).

Some scholars who do not agree with this Conversion theory cite the following lines from the *Conte dou Graal* to prove that Chrétien detested the Jewish people, and therefore could not have been sympathetic to them, either as individuals or as a group: "The wicked Jews through their envy, who should be slain like dogs, did ill to themselves and great good to us when they raised Him upon the Cross. They damned themselves and gave us salvation" (vss. 6292–96). However, in this passage Chrétien is speaking specifically of the Jews who crucified Christ. He is not alluding to Jewish people in general, or to his Jewish neighbors in Champagne who—we suggest—he would have liked to persuade to throw off their old allegiance.

CHAPTER 11

Epilogue

I N these pages we have begun each chapter with what Chrétien says about himself or the work in question. This is of first importance in every case. After that the reader may choose for himself among the many opinions that have been expressed. But there are certain general questions on which, after weighing the matters very carefully, an interested reader should make personal judgment. Since Chrétien was unquestionably a clerk, with simple tonsure at least, during his writing career, he must have had school training—perhaps even some advanced study at a *Studium* such as that at Troyes. Do you believe that he was receptive to folklore on a considerable scale, or did he get most of his material from written sources? Just how important were influences from the contiguous civilizations: from the Celts, the Byzantines, the Jews? Do you think that Chrétien, from his position as a Christian cleric in the middle of Champagne, would have had points of contact with and inclination toward the Albigensians, the Muslims, the Gnostic sects, and other Oriental religions and cults?

We know, of course, that library facilities, where they existed at all, were very poor. Yet we must not forget that the mid-twelfth century saw a Renaissance in teaching, a great new interest in dialectic, in defining things such as Love and the meaning of Light in accord with the newly acquired insight gained from some of Plato and Aristotle. There was new material on science coming up from Spain and from Italy. Many men had come home after harrowing experiences of travel, on foot and on horseback, to the Holy Land, to Italy, and to Spain. Many others had contacts in England. A certain amount of Subjectivism, of personal expression of opinion, was very much in the air—and much of this took the form of sentiment.

Men were not good linguists at this time; but Latin was thoroughly learned by most of the clerks. Thanks largely to Anglo-Norman activity, French could be used rather widely. I doubt that many French or Anglo-Normans knew more than a few words of Celtic. (And yet the poet who wrote the Provençal *Flamenca* does mention that the hostess at Guillem's lodging house spoke Burgundian, French, German, and Breton [vss. 1924–25]. Greek too was known by almost no one in the West (excepting, of course, in southern Italy). Those, such as the Templars, who knew Arabic resided for the most part in the Arabic-speaking countries. The Jews had a culture of their own, and they could also be used as intermediaries in drawing upon the Arabs.

Reflection on these many streams of influence will make it easier for you to come to a decision for yourself on what Chrétien meant—what he wanted to express.

Some critics today assume that the psychology of the twelfth century did not differ much from the reactions which govern most of our behavior today. Is this really true? Medieval men had the same physiological responses that we have, but their environment, their experiences, their taboos, their licence, and the books which they studied and read, made them different people. They would not understand our modern world and, only too often, I am afraid, we do not understand theirs.

Notes And References

Chapter One

1. This and all subsequent references will be to the editions of Chrétien's works published in the "Classiques français du moyen âge" (CFMA) series, edited by Mario Roques (*Erec and Enide, Lancelot,* and *Yvain*), Alexandre Micha (*Cligés*), and Maurice Wilmotte (*Guillaume d'Angleterre*). I have used the edition of the *Perceval* prepared by William J. Roach. Complete bibliographical information on these and other editions of Chrétien is to be found in the bibliography to the present volume.

2. The best edition is that of Mary Williams, *Gerbert de Montreuil: La Continuation de Perceval,* nos. 28 and 50 in the CFMA series.

3. A good edition of the *Lais* of Marie de France is that by Alfred Ewert for "Blackwell's French Texts" (Oxford: B. Blackwell, 1952).

4. The discussion seemed to have been resolved by Maurice Wilmotte in "Chrétien de Troyes et le Conte de *Guillaume d'Angleterre,*" *Romania,* XLVI (1920), 1–38, who determined that our Chrétien de Troyes did indeed compose the *Guillaume.* This opinion was opposed, however, notably in 1931 by F. J. Tanquery in "Chrétien de Troyes, est-il l'auteur de *Guillaume d'Angleterre?*" who felt the *Guillaume* to be a poor imitation of Chrétien's work (in *Romania,* LVII [1931], 75–116).

5. The two lyrics are nos. 121 and 1664 in Gaston Raynaud's *Bibliographie des chansonniers français des XIIe et XIVe siecles* (2 vols.; Paris: F. Vieweg, 1884). They are also reproduced in Wendelin Foerster's *Kristian von Troyes: Wörterbuch zu seinen sämtlichen Werken* (Halle, 1914), pp. 205–9. Note that this work was reissued in 1933, but minus the lengthy introduction which contains these lyrics as well as Foerster's mature comments on Chrétien's life and works.

6. The standard edition of the *Ovide moralisé* is that by C. de Boer (Amsterdam: Muller, 1915) in five volumes; this scholar also did a separate edition of the *Philomena* (Paris: Geuthner, 1909). On the *Philomena,* see especially F. Zaman, *L'attribution de 'Philomena' à Chrétien de Troyes* (Amsterdam: H. J. Paris, 1928), who does not assign it to Chrétien; and Ernest Hoepffner, "La *Philomena* de

Chrétien de Troyes," *Romania*, LVII (1931), 13,74, who does. Also De Boer again in *Romania*, XLI.

7. Gaston Paris' comments on Chrétien are to be found mostly in his review of Wendelin Foerster's edition of the *Cligés*. These have been reprinted by Mario Roques in *Gaston Paris Mélanges de littérature française du moyen âge* (Paris: Champion 1910), which is the source we shall draw upon (esp. pp. 244–68).

8. This *Tristan* is mentioned by the anonymous author of the *Roman de Renart* in the Ernest Martin edition, Branch II, v. 5 (Strasbourg: K. J. Trübner and Paris: E. Leroux, 1882–87). A new edition of the *Roman de Renart* is being prepared by Mario Roques for the CFMA series (nos. 78–18, 81, 85, 88, 90). In a *conte dévot* there is another mention of a *Tristan* by Li Kievres (*Foerster Festschrift*, Halle, 1902).

9. This summary of Foerster's ideas about the life and works of Chrétien was taken from the introduction to the 1914 edition of his *Kristian von Troyes: Wörterbuch* (see n. 5 above); we have drawn particularly from pp. 21–46.

10. In *Le Moyen Age*, II (1889), 188–91.

11. The complete title of his oft-quoted study is *Chrétien de Troyes: Leben und Werke des altfranzösischen Epikers* (Graz-Köln: H. Böhlau, 1954).

12. L. A. Vigneras, "Chrétien de Troyes Rediscovered," *Modern Philology*, XXXII (1934–35), 341–42.

13. This book, designed for the layman as well as for the specialist, belongs to the collection *Connaissance des Lettres* (Paris: Hatier-Boivin, 1957). See also Jean Misrahi, "Symbolism and Allegory in Arthurian Romance," *Romance Philology*, XVII (1964), 555–70.

14. See also Loomis' *Celtic Myth and Arthurian Romance* (New York: Columbia University Press, 1927).

15. Anthime Fourrier, "Encore la chronologie des oeuvres de Chrétien de Troyes," *Bulletin bibliographique de la société internationale arthurienne*, II (1950), 69–88. An up-to-date view of this dating by Fourrier is in Jean Misrahi, "More Light on the Chronology of Chrétien de Troyes," *ibid.*, XI (1959), 89–120. There have been many different suggestions on the relative chronology of the works of Chrétien. See Lucy M. Gay (*Romanic Review*, XIV, 47–60), Foster E. Guyer (*Modern Philology*, XXVI, 257–77), Stefan Hofer (*Zeits. für franz. Spr. und Lit.* LX, 335–43, 441–55).

16. See our paper, "Norman Literature and Wace," which was delivered at the Center for Medieval and Renaissance Studies at

the University of California, Los Angeles, in April, 1964, and was printed in *Medieval Secular Literature: Four Essays* (Berkeley and Los Angeles: University of California Press, 1965), edited by William Matthews. The same method is used in *Samuel Pepys in Paris and Other Essays* (Chapel Hill: University of North Carolina Press, 1954).

17. A more complete study of the area of Troyes in the twelfth century is to be found in the first chapter of my *Chrétien, Troyes, and the Grail* (with Sister M. Amelia Klenke, O.P.) (Chapel Hill: University of North Carolina Press, 1959). On Peter Comestor at Troyes, see Saralyn R. Daly in *Speculum*, XXXII (1957), 65.

18. Some of the results of his research have been published in "The Court of Champagne as a Literary Center," *Speculum*, XXXVI, 551–91. See especially pp. 561–63; others have been sent to me in personal correspondence.

19. In "The Name *Chrétien* and Perspectives on the Grail," *Romance Notes*, VI, no. 2 (1965), 209–14. A much more detailed discussion of the frequency of occurrence of the name "Chrétien" will be found in the third chapter of *Chrétien, Troyes, and the Grail* (see n. 17 above).

20. Gertrude Schoepperle, *Tristan and Isolt, A Study of the Sources of the Romance* (2 vols.; Frankfort and London, 1913).

21. A variant version of Geoffrey of Monmouth's *Historia regum Brittaniae*, was prepared for the Medieval Academy of America by Jacob Hammer (Cambridge, Mass., 1951). There is also an English translation by Sebastian Evans (London: J. M. Dent and Co., 1904).

22. D. W. Robertson, "Chrétien's Cligés and the Ovidian Spirit," *Comparative Literature*, VII (1955), 32–42; Barbara Nelson Sargent, "L'autre chez Chrétien de Troyes," *Cahiers de Civilisation médiévale*, X (1967), 199–205. We should like to add to this a similarity with the story of Job: relative prosperity, trials, and reward.

23. For this see Julian Harris' Introduction to *Chrétien de Troyes* (Dell [n.d.] in the Laurel Language Library).

24. Alice M. Colby, *The Portrait in Twelfth-Century French Literature: an Example of the Stylistic Originality of Chrétien de Troyes* (Genève: Droz, 1965), Lorenza Maranini, *Personaggi e immagini nell'opera di Chretien de Troyes* (Milano: Varese, 1966), and Jean Györy, "Prolégomènes à une imagerie de Chrétien de Troyes," *Cahiers de civilisation médiévale*, X (1967), 361–84.

Chapter Two

1. The following works might be consulted with profit. Charles H. Haskins, *The Renaissance of the Twelfth Century* (Cambridge: Harvard University Press, 1927; paperbacked, Cleveland and New York: Meridian Books, 1962); Frederick B. Artz, *The Mind of the Middle Ages* (2nd ed.; New York: Knopf, 1954); Urban T. Holmes, "Transitions in European Education" in Marshall Clagett, Gaines Post, and Robert Reynolds (eds.), *Twelfth-Century Europe and the Foundations of Modern Society* (Madison: University of Wisconsin Press, 1961), pp. 15–38; *idem,* "The Idea of a Twelfth-Century Renaissance," *Speculum* XXVI (1951), 643–51; Ernst Robert Curtius, *European Literature and the Latin Middle Ages* (New York: Pantheon Books, 1953); Erich Auerbach, *Mimesis, the Representation of Reality in Western Literature* (New York: Doubleday Anchor Books, 1957). For daily life of the twelfth century the student should use Alwin Schultz, *Das Höfische Leben zur Zeit der Minnesinger,* (2 vols.; Leipzig: Verlag von S. Hirzel, 1889). See also Urban T. Holmes, *A History of Old French Literature from the Origins to 1300* (New York: Russell and Russell, 1962).

2. The historical perspective of the time is given from *The Cambridge Medieval History* (6 vols.; New York: Macmillan, 1911–36); Ernest Lavisse, *Histoire de France Illustrée* (Paris: Hachette [n.d.]), Vol. III, première parties; see also Auguste Molinier, *Les Sources de l'histoire de France depuis les origines aux guerres d'Italie (1494)* (6 vols.; Paris: A. Picard, 1901–6).

3. C. de Boer (ed.), *Philomena, Conte raconté d'après Ovide par Chrétien de Troyes* (Paris: 1909).

4. The discussion of the origins of the romance form has been extensive. See especially Edmond Faral, *Recherches sur les sources latines des contes et romans courtois du moyen age* (Paris: Champion, 1913); M. Wilmotte, *Origines du roman en France, l'évolution du sentiment romanesque jusqu'en 1240* (Paris: Boivin, [n.d.]); Reto R. Bezzola, *Les Origines et la formation de la littérature courtoise en Occident* (Paris: Champion, 1944). For more detailed study, see the sections on the origin of the romance in Robert Bossuat, *Manuel bibliographique de la littérature française du moyen âge* (Melun: Librairie d'Argences, 1951). There are supplemental issues, covering 1949–53 and 1954–60, respectively; also D. C. Cabeen, *Critical Bibliographies of French Literature,* Vol. I, ed. Urban T. Holmes, *The Mediaeval Period* (enlarged ed.; Syracuse: Syracuse University Press, 1952).

5. P. xliv of her Introduction to *Les œuvres poétiques de Baudri de Bourgueil* (Paris: Champion, 1926). A complete edition of Baudri (Baldericus) is found in J. P. Migne, *Patrologiae cursus completus,* Vol. CLXVI.

6. Most of this material on the new Romantic spirit has been summarized from R. W. Southern, *The Making of the Middle Ages* (New Haven: Yale University Press, 1953).

7. Southern, pp. 243, 246, and 222.

8. For this matter on the concept of Love in the twelfth century we have used Peter Dronke, *Medieval Latin and the Rise of the European Love-lyric* (Oxford: Clarendon Press, 1965), Vol. I, chap. II. Perhaps we are a little rash in sketching this outline of technical material here; but the reader will glimpse from this something about the origins of Courtly Love, about Italian *dolce stil nuovo,* and indeed about an important twelfth century interpretation of the biblical Song of Songs.

9. For all of this see Karl Kinzel, *Lamprechts Alexander* (Halle: Verlag der Buchhandlung des Waisenhauses, 1884).

10. Walter Ziltener, *Chrétien und die Aeneis eine Untersuchung des Einflusses von Vergil auf Chretien von Troyes* (Bern diss., Graz; Köln, 1957). See also Foster E. Guyer, "The influence of Ovid on Crestien de Troyes," *Romanic Review* XII (1921), and his *Romance in the Making* (New York: Vanni, 1954).

11. The question of whether there was some sort of literary treatment of Arthurian material prior to Chrétien rests on the dating of the sculptures in the tympanum of the famous north door at Modena Cathedral in Italy. R. S. Loomis insisted that these sculptures, some of which have Arthurian names, were earlier than 1130. See *Romanic Review,* XXXII (1941), 3–38. With all due respect for Loomis' arguments, a principal difficulty is that we cannot believe the romance form was in use at that early date. Of course, some popular chronicle form, such as we must accept for Alberic's *Alexander* poem in Franco-Provençal, could have been in use. It seems to us that in his explanation of the origins of the romance, Edmond Faral sidestepped completely the problems of Alberic's poem and of the Modena sculpture. For dating of the Modena sculpture later than 1150, see G. H. Gerould in *Speculum,* X (1935), 355–76.

Chapter Three

1. The most accessible editions of the works of Ovid are those in the "Loeb Classical Library" series, Cambridge: Harvard Uni-

versity Press, and London: William Heinmann Ltd. These provide the Latin text and English translation on facing pages. For Ovidian influence on Chrétien, see Foster E. Guyer, "The Influence of Ovid in Chrétien de Troyes," Romanic Review, XII (1921), 97–134 & 216–47. See also our chap. v, n. 5.

2. A modern edition of Hyginus is *Hygini Gavulae*, ed. H. I. Rose (Leyden: A. W. Sijthoff, 1963).

3. *Rheinisches Museum*, 1892, Ergänzungshilf, 3.

4. Paris' arguments are to be found in his well-known article in the *Journal des Savants*, reprinted by Mario Roques. See our chap. i, n. 7. Foerster's position is set forth in the introduction to his edition of the *Cligés*. Alexandre Micha, "Tristan et Cligés" (*Neophilologus*, XXXVI [1952], 1–10), felt that the *"sens"* of Chrétien's lost Tristan poem could be determined from his attitude toward Tristan and Iseut in the *Cligés*.

5. Stith Thompson, *Motif-Index of Folk-Literature* (6 vols.; Bloomington: Indiana University Press, 1932–36).

6. Published by Bartina Wind (Genève: Droz, 1969).

7. See the translation by Thomas Forester of *The Historical Works of Giraldus Cambrensis* (London and New York: G. Bell, 1892) and *The Itinerary through Wales and the Description of Wales* (London: J. M. Dent & Co.; New York: E. P. Dutton & Co., [1908]).

8. Gaston Paris accepted the *Philomena* as a work of our Chrétien in "Un poème retrouvé de Chrétien de Troyes," *Romania*, XIII (1884), 399–400. Foerster's objections can be found in the introduction to his edition of the *Cligés*. See Raphael Levy, "Old French *Goz* and Chrestiiens li Gois," *PMLA*, XLVI (1931), 312–30, and in "Etat présent des études sur l'attribution de *"Philomenia,"* *Les Lettres romanes*, V (1951), 46 52; as well as in the articles mentioned in our chap. i, n. 6.

9. See our chap. i, n. 5.

10. This poem is no. 29 in *The Songs of Bernart de Ventadorn*, ed. Stephen G. Nichols, Jr. ("UNC Studies in the Romance Languages and Literatures," 39 [Chapel Hill: University of North Carolina Press, 1962]).

11. Carl Appel (ed.), *Raimbaut von Orange* (Berlin: Weidmann, 1928).

Chapter Four

Albert Pauphilet, "Nouveaux fragments manuscrits de Chrétien de Troyes," *Romania*, LXIII (1937), 310–23. He reproduced these photographically in *Le Manuscrit d'Annonay* (Paris, 1934).

2. See O. Jodogne, "Fragments de Mons.I. Erec et Enide de Chrétien de Troyes," *Les Lettres romanes*, IV (1950), 311–13.

3. Reported by Antoine Thomas in his article "Fragment de l' "Erec" de Chrétien de Troies" (*Romania*, XLIII [1914], 253–55).

4. See R. R. Bezzola, *Les Origines et la formation de la littérature courtoise en Occident (500–1200)* (Paris: E. Champion, 1944).

5. See their studies referred to in nn. 11 and 15 of our chap. i.

6. A recent edition of Wace's *Le Roman de Brut* is that prepared by Ivor Arnold, in two volumes, for the *Société des anciens textes français* (SATF), 1938–40.

7. In "The Plot Structure in Four Romances of Chrestien de Troyes" (*Studies in Philology*, L [1953], 1–15).

8. The precise connotation of the word *conjointure* has been the subject for some scholarly discussion. See D. W. Robertson, "Some Medieval Literary Terminology, with special reference to Chrétien de Troyes," *Studies in Philology*, XLVIII (1951), 669–92; and William A. Nitze, "Conjointure in *Erec* vs. 14," *Modern Language Notes*, LXIX (1954), 180–81.

9. We have mentioned on p. 25 above that D. W. Robertson thinks that in his treatment of love in the *Cligés*, Chrétien was being ironical throughout. Thomas C. Rumble in *The Breton Lays in Middle English* (Detroit: Wayne State University Press, 1965), p. xvi, is more extreme and refers to this poem as a parody. I am sure this statement was made *en passant*, without serious reflection.

10. See the chapter entitled "Le merveilleux et ses sources dans les descriptions des romans" in Edmond Faral's *Recherches sur les sources latines des contes et romans courtois du moyen âge* (Paris: Champion, 1913).

11. *Arthurian Tradition and Chrétien de Troyes* (New York: Columbia University Press, 1949).

12. R. Harris, "The White Stag in Chrétien's *Erec et Enide*," *French Studies*, X (1956), 56–61.

13. This has been published by Migne in the *Patrologiae cursus completus*, Vol. CLXXIX.

14. These names still require considerable study. See, however, R. S. Loomis' *Arthurian Tradition and Chrétien de Troyes;* R. Harris, "Et Liconaus ot non ses pere," *Medium Aevum*, XXVI (1957), 32–35; Jean Frappier, *Chrétien de Troyes: l'homme et l'œuvre* (Paris: Hatier-Boivin, 1957), p. 40 ff.

15. See his "Kritische Bemerkungen zum *Lai de Guingamor*," *Romanische Forschungen*, LXV (1954), 360–77, esp. pp. 375–77.

16. Richard William Southern, *The Making of the Middle Ages*

(New Haven: Yale University Press, 1953), p. 246. See also M. Mills, "The Huntsman and the Dwarf in *Erec* and *Li beaus desconus*," *Romania*, LXXXVII (1966), 33–58; Z. P. Zaddy, "Pourquoi Erec se décide-t-il à partir en voyage avec Enide?" *CCM*, VII (1964), 179–85.

17. For other interpretations of the *matière* and *sens* of this poem, see especially Carol C. Bang, "Emotions and attitudes in Chrestiens de Troyes' *Erec et Enide* and Hartman von Aue's *Erec der Wanderaere*," *PMLA*, LVII (1942), 297–326; William A. Nitze, "The Romance of Erec, son of Lot," *Modern Philology*, X (1912–13), 445–89; *idem*, "Erec's treatment of Enide," *Romanic Review*, X (1919), 26–37; E. S. Sheldon, "Why does Chrétien's Erec treat Enide so harshly?," *Romanic Review*, V (1914), 433–50; E. Philipot, "Un épisode d'Erec et Enide: la Joie de la Cour, Mabon l'Enchanteur," *Romania*, XXV (1896), 258–94.

18. See, among others, William A. Nitze's "Yvain and the Myth of the Fountain" in *Speculum*, XXX (1955), 170–79.

Chapter Five

1. Some may wonder why we do not write *Cligès* instead of *Cligés*. The grave accent is a *modern* French accent mark and we are not modernizing such names. The acute accent, although not used frequently in the Middle Ages, *did* exist as a distinguishing stroke.

2. Foerster, *op, cit.*, chap. i, n. 5. See also A. G. Van Hamel, "Cligés et Tristan," *Romania*, XXVI (1904), 465–89.

3. "Studi di Filologia Moderna," (Turin: Bottega d'Erasmo, 1963).

4. Ziltener, *op. cit.* (See chap. ii, n. 7), 76–78 and *passim*. On Chrétien and Ovid, see Alexandre Micha, "Eneas et Cligés" in *Mélanges Ernest Hoepffner* (Paris, 1949), 237–43; and D. W. Robertson, Jr., "Chrétien's Cligés and the Ovidian Spirit," *Comparative Literature*, VII (1955), 32–42.

5. Printed by Walter Benary in his *Salomon et Marcolfus* (Heidelberg: Sammlung Mittellateinische Texte, 1914), 48–51. The version found in the thirteenth-century *Marques de Rome* was probably circulating in substantially the same form in the twelfth century.

6. On Averroës, see A. C. Crombie, *Medieval and Early Modern Science* (New York: Doubleday Anchor Books, 1959), I, 111–12. For the Church colors, see Massey H. Shepherd, *The Oxford American Prayer Book Commentary* (New York: Oxford University

Press, 1950), Commentary on pp. xlvi–xlix. The symbolism in these four colors may run even deeper. In Alchemy, black was referred to as the raven's head; the "stone of whiteness" is supposed to be capable of transmuting other metals into silver; the "stone of redness" transmutes metals into gold; the "Green Lion" is also important. Thus the phases of alchemy work are expressed by different colors. Grillot de Girry, *A Pictorial Anthology of Witchcraft, Magic, and Alchemy*, trans. J. Courtnay Locke (Chicago and New York: University Books, 1958). Convinced as we are that the symbolism intended here by Chrétien was Christian, we quote this Alchemy reference merely for the sake of completeness.

7. J. D. Bruce, *op. cit.*, I, 211–12.

8. See Galia Millard's edition of *Calendre, Les Empereors de Rome* (Ann Arbor, Michigan: University of Michigan Press, 1957).

9. E. C. Armstrong and others (eds.), *The Mediaeval French Roman d'Alexandre* (Princeton: Elliott Monographs, 1937), II, vss. 583, 688, etc.

10. (Poitiers: Centre d'Etudes supérieures de civilisation médiévale, 1962). Cligés as a name is referred to in eleven works, Fenice in three, and Thessala in the *Prose Tristan*.

11. Facsimile edition by Henry Roseman Lang (New York, 1926).

Chapter Six

1. English translation of Ulrich's *Lanzelet* by Kenneth G. T. Webster, with Introduction and Notes by R. S. Loomis (New York: Columbia University Press, 1951). See also the article by Stefan Hofer, "Der Lanzelet des Ulrich von Zatzikhoven und seine französische Quelle," *Zeitschrift für romanische Philologie*, LXXV (1959), 1–36.

2. See their jointly authored *Lancelot and Guenevere, a Study on the Origins of Courtly Love* ("Modern Philology Monographs of the University of Chicago" [Chicago: University of Chicago Press, 1930]). See also F. D. Kelly, *Sens et conjointure dans le Chevalier de la Charrette* (The Hague: Mouton, 1966).

3. The contemporary "handbook" for the conceptions and practices of courtly love was the *De Arte Honnesti Amandi* of Andreas Capellanus, who composed it for the court of Marie de Champagne at Troyes (English trans. *The Art of Courtly Love*, by John Jay Perry [New York: Columbia University Press, 1941]). On the treatment of courtly love in Chrétien's *Lancelot*, see P. Jonin, "Le

vasselage de Lancelot dans le 'Conte de la Charrette,' " *Le Moyen Age*, LVIII (1952), 281–98; and Charles Foulon, "Les deux humiliations de Lancelot," *Bulletin bibliographique de la Société internationale arthurienne*, no. 8 (1956), 79–90.

4. Albert Pauphilet, *op. cit.* (chap ii, n. 9). Pauphilet is rather persistently haunted by the idea that the Land of the Dead is reflected in Chrétien's romances. To be sure, there is a Celtic motif (F 160.0.2) in the Thompson Index in which Celtic Otherworld and the Land of the Dead are equated.

5. Tom Peete Cross, *Motif Index of Early Irish Literature* (Bloomington: Indiana University Publications, Folklore Series no 17, [1952]), entries F 842.2.3.2.

6. See also: Douglas Kelly, *Sens and Conjointure in the Chevalier de la Charette*, (The Hague: Mouton & Co., 1966) and J. Mandel, "Elements in the *Charette* World: the Father-Son Relationship," *Modern Philology*, LXII (1964), 97–104.

Chapter Seven

1. Eugene Vinaver's presidential address before The Modern Humanities Research Association in 1966.

2. E. Kölbing, *Ivens Saga* (Altnordische Saga-Bibliothek, Vol. VII, 1898). See W. Foerster in *Kristian von Troyes: Wörterbuch*, p. 130.

3. *Romanic Review*, XVI (1925), 43–53.

4. In the Welsh *Brut* of the Red Book of Hergest we find "Mureif, the land which is called by another name Rheged." Uryen, Leu, and Arawn are the names given here for these sons of Kinnmarcus. Geoffrey of Monmouth was probably rendered into Welsh shortly after 1200. The Red Book *Bruts* are thought to be closely related to the earliest version. See John Rhys and J. G. Evans, *The Text of the Bruts of the Red Book of Hergest* (Oxford, 1890).

5. In Geoffrey, *Historia Regum Britanniae*, ed. E. Faral (3 vols.; Paris: Champion, 1929), the names are Anguselus, Urianus, and Loth (III, 237).

6. *Ibid.*, II, 263.

7. H. Pedersen, *Vergl. Gramm. d. Kelt. Spr.* (Göttingen, 1909–11), I, 73, 101.

8. J. Morris Jones in *Y Cymmrodor*, XXVIII (1918).

9. Giraldus, *op cit.* (chap. iii, n. 6), 32–33.

10. Ed. Hugo Andresen (Heilbronn: Henninger, 1879).

11. *Historia Orientalis et Occidentalis*, Liber II, chap. xcii.

12. *An Inquiry into the Structural Style and Originality of Chrestien's Yvain* ("Catholic University of America Studies in Romance Languages and Literatures," LVII [Washington, 1958], p. 73. See also Faith Lyons, "Sentiment et rhetorique dans l'*Yvain*," *Romania*, LXXXIII (1962), 370–77.

13. Introduction to André Mary's modern French translation of the *Yvain* (New York: Dell Publishing Co., 1963). But chiefly see his "The Role of the Lion in Chrétien de Troyes's Yvain," PMLA, LXIV (1949), 1143–63.

14. *Symbolisme médiéval* (Istanbul: Matbaasi, 1956), 126, 222.

15. (Rolls Series, 1963), vol. 34, pp. 130–31.

16. MS. B.N. 25.566, fol. 183 r. Mrs. Christoph Bender has a new edition of this in preparation.

17. For Max Luria see *infra*.

18. Erich Auerbach, *Mimesis,* tr. Willard Trask (Doubleday Anchor Books: New York), chapter VI.

19. *Le legs du moyen-âge* (Melun, 1950), 150.

20. *Chrétien de Troyes* (Paris: Hatier-Boivin, 1957). chapter VI.

Chapter Eight

1. Gustav Gröber, *Grundriss der romanischen Philologie* (2 vols.; Strasbourg: Karl J. Trübner, 1888–1902), II, 524.

2. See *Romania*, III, 507 and VIII, 315–20.

3. Madrid: La Sociedad de Bibliófilos españoles, 1878).

4. *Op. cit.,* 524.

5. In "Forerunners, Congeners, and Derivatives of the Eustace Legend," *PMLA*, XIX (1904), 335–448.

6. *Op. cit.*

7. We have converted Chrétien's place names, Bristot, Galveide, Sorlinc, and Quatenasse into Bristol, Galloway, Stirling, and Caithness. It is quite evident that these are the places intended.

8. For example, Charles Foulon, "Les tendences aristocratiques dans le roman de *Guillaume d'Angleterre*," *Romania*, LXXI (1950), 222–37.

9. H. E. Butler, (ed.), *The Chronicle of Jocelin of Brakelonde* (T. Nelson, 1949), p. 48.

10. R. L. Graeme Ritchie, *Crétien and Scotland* (Oxford, 1952).

Chapter Nine

1. Charles Beaulieux, *Histoire de l'orthographe française* (2 vols.; Paris: Honore Champion, 1927), I, 42ff.

2. Jacques-Charles Brunet, *Manuel du libraire et de l'amateur de livres* (6 vols. and 2 suppl.; Paris: F. de Nobelle, 1820), IV, 487.

3. *Crestien von Troyes Conte del Graal (Perceval li Galois)*. *Abdruck der Hs. Paris français 794*. Nicht im Buchhandel. (Freiburg i. Baden, 1909). There was a second edition in 1912.

4. Halle: Niemeyer, 1932.

5. Genève: Librairie Droz, 1959.

6. "Wauchier de Denain," *Romania*, XXXII (1903), 583–86.

7. So named by Bédier and Jessie L. Weston in *Romania*, XXXV (1906), 497–530, in which they collaborated and published the section of Gerbert's continuation relating the adventures of Tristan.

8. *The Evolution of Arthurian Romance from the Beginnings down to the Year 1300* (2 vols.; Göttingen, 1923), I, 219–68.

9. *Ibid.*, pp. 243.

10. See Alfred Nutt, *Studies on the Legend of the Holy Grail, with especial reference to the hypothesis of its Celtic origin* (London: Publications of the Folklore Society, no. XXIII, 1888), pp. 100ff.

11. *The Legend of Sir Perceval; Studies upon its origin, development, and position in the Arthurian cycle* (2 vols.; London: Grimm Library nos. 17–19, 1906–9). See especially Vol. II, 1909.

12. Cambridge: The University Press, 1920.

13. *PMLA*, XXIV (1909), 365 ff.

14. It is not our intention to counter any of the theories presented in this chapter; but we can state positively that the Grail is always referred to as similar to an *escuelle,* and that the medieval *escuelle* is not a platter—it is bowl-like in shape. See our chap. x, p. 166; also p. 140.

15. *La légende arthurienne et le Graal* (Paris: Les Presses universitaires, 1952), p. 314.

16. *L'Islam et le Graal* (Paris: Editions Denoel, 1957), pp. 16–18.

17. In *The Literary Review*, I (1957), 57–71.

18. Paris: Les Cahiers du Sud, 1951.

19. *Atti Accademici dei Lincei*, CCCLVIII (1961), 126ff.

20. Manchester: Manchester University Press, 1966.

21. This theory is outlined in *Zeitschrift für romanische Philologie*, LXXIX (1963), 335–42. Most important is their *The Krater and the Grail: Hermetic Studies of the Parzival* (Urbana: University of Illinois Press, 1965). See review of this by Leo Pollman in *Cahiers de Civilisation médiévale*, X (1967), 241–42.

22. The Kahanes have taken this translation from Adlinton and Gaselee, *Apuleius, Golden Ass* (Loeb Classical Library), 53.

23. *Cahiers de Civilisation médiévale*, X (1967), 207–19.

24. I. L. Foster in Loomis' *Arthurian Literature in the Middle Ages*, pp. 199–205. Consult also: Helen Adolf, *Visio Pacis: Holy City and Grail: an Attempt at an Inner History of the Grail Legend.* (State College: Pennsylvania State University Press, 1960); Jean Marx, *Nouvelles recherches sur le cycle arthurien: Origines et développement de la légende du Graal* (Paris: Klincksieck, 1965); Francis Carmody, "Sources orientales du *Perceval*," RLC, XXXIX (1965), 497–545; Istvan Frank, "Le cortège du Graal et le relique de Saint Denis," *Romania*, LXXXII (1961), 241–44; Helmut Hatzfeld, "Deuten Stilelements in Chretiens *Perceval* auf eine strukturelle Einheit?" *Medium Aevum Romanicum*, XXXII (1963), 140–60; Stanton de V. Hoffmann, "The Structure of the *Conte del Graal*," *Romanic Review*, LII (1961), 81–98; Faith Lyons, "Beauté et lumière dans le *Perceval* de Chrétien de Troyes," *Romania*, LXXXVI (1965), 104–11; D.D.R. Owen, "Radiance in the Graal Castle," *Romania*, LXXXIII (1962), 108–17; Carlo Pellegrini, "Per l'interpretazione del *Perceval* di Chrétien de Troyes," *Varia umanità*, XXXIX (1963), 109–18.

Chapter Ten

1. See Louis-Fernand Flutre, *Table des noms propres . . . figurant dans les romans du moyen age* (Poitiers: Centre d'Etudes supérieures de civilisation médiévale, 1962).
2. *Chrétien, Troyes, and the Grail* (Chapel Hill: University of North Carolina Press, 1959); also, Sister M. Amelia Klenke, O.P., *A New Interpretation of Chrétien's Conte del Graal* (Chapel Hill: UNC Studies in the Romance Languages and Literatures, 1948).
3. *Dictionnaire des lettres* (Paris, 1964).
4. "Le Graal de Chrétien et la demoiselle au Graal," *Romania*, LCCVI (1955), 1–27.
5. See Helaine Newstead, "The Blancheflor-Perceval Question again," *Romance Philology*, VII (1953), 171–75.
6. Jean Frappier in R. S. Loomis, *op. cit.*, 265–66, 269.
7. R. S. Loomis, *op. cit.*, 251–62.
8. In R. S. Loomis, *op. cit.*, 265–66, 269.
9. See n. 1 above. Also Wace's *Brut* vv. 11063–1169: "In that island there were giants, no other people lived there. The giants were very large in body, grown beyond the size of other people. I cannot tell you their names except one . . . Goemagog who was their Lord." *Brut*, ed. Ivor Arnold (Paris: SATF, 1938).
10. Migne, *Pat. Lat.*, Vol. CLXXXIII.

11. In 1204 Gerald the Welshman, who was visiting Rome as a pilgrim, says that he saw in the Treasury of the Pope's Lateran Palace at Rome: the ark of the covenant, the tables of the law, the golden urn of manna, the rod of Aaron, the seven-branched candelabrum, the holy table and cloth. (*Speculum Ecclesiae*, IV, 2–6 (ed. Brewer, Rolls Series), IV, 269–80. We are not arguing that these were truly the sacred talismans of the Temple at Jerusalem, which had been destroyed—but apparently Gerald and most every one else believed that they were authentic. This lends considerable weight to our suggestion that in the last quarter of the twelfth century it was considered obvious that the sacred objects of the Old Testament could pass to the New.

12. Trans. G. Ryan and C. Ripperger (London: Longmans, Green, 1941), p. 191.

13. *The Jerusalem Bible* (Garden City: Doubleday, 1966). Sister Amelia's ideas on the influence of the Song of Songs on the description of the Grail Procession are drawn from a paper which has not yet been printed.

14. Migne, *Pat. Lat.*, Vol. CCXIII, cols. 814–15.

15. Professor Loomis has often cited this quotation (in part only.)

Selected Bibliography

1. General

BEZZOLA, R. R. *Les origines et la formation de la littérature courtoise en Occident (500–1200)*. 3 vols. so far; Paris: Champion, 1944. Vast amount of material; perhaps a bit diffuse.

BRUCE, JAMES DOUGLAS. *The Evolution of Arthurian Romance, from the beginnings down to the year 1300*. Göttingen, 1923; 2nd ed. by ALFONS HILKA, Baltimore: Johns Hopkins University Press, 1928. Basic statement of the problems, with many useful summaries.

CHAMBERS, E. K. *Arthur of Britain*. London: Sidgwick and Jackson, 1927. Useful for surveying origins of Arthurian Romance; contains some Latin texts.

FARAL, EDMOND. *La légende arthurienne*, 3 vols.; Paris: Champion, 1929. Valuable collection of materiel, including a Latin text of Geoffrey of Monmouth; presents extreme anti-Celtic and anti-folklore point of view.

LOOMIS, ROGER SHERMAN and others, *Arthurian Literature in the Middle Ages*. Oxford: Oxford University Press, 1959. Collective volume with chapters contributed by various experts; most important reference. Chapters contributed by Loomis himself rather extreme in their exposition of Celtic origins.

2. Bibliography

BOSSUAT, ROBERT. *Manuel bibliographique de la littérature française du moyen âge*. Melun: Libraire d'Argences, 1951, with two supplements. Fine body of material, although critical comments are few.

Bulletin bibliographique de la Société internationale arthurienne. Paris, 1949. Standard bibliographical reference; contains articles also.

CABEEN, D. C. *A Critical Bibliography of French Literature*. Rev. ed.; Syracuse: Syracuse University Press, 1952. Items on Arthur-

ian Romance (I, 101–23) by JOHN J. PARRY; on Chrétien and
the Tristan legend (I, 129–30) by HELENE NEWSTEAD; on the
Grail theme (I, 130–36) by WILLIAM ROACH.

PARRY, JOHN J., SCHLAUCH, MARGARET, and others. *A Bibliography
of Critical Arthurian Literature.* 2 vols.; New York: Modern
Language Association, 1931–36. First volume (or issue) contains titles for the years 1922–20; second issue has items for
1931–36. This bibliography began as a supplement to the titles
listed by J. D. Bruce (see above); beginning with the June
issue of 1940, Parry printed an annual bibliography in the
Modern Language Quarterly, through 1953; this task was continued by Paul A. Brown through 1963.

3. Editions

*Christian von Troyes, Sämtliche erhaltene Werke, nach allen bekann-
ten Handschriften herausgegeben von Wendelin Foerster.* 4
volumes; Halle; Niemeyer, 1884–99. Vol. I (1884) *Cligés;* Vol.
II (1887) *Der Löwenritter* (*Yvain*); Vol. III (1890) *Erec and
Enide;* Vol. IV (1899) *Der Karrenritter* (*Lancelot*) *und das
Wilhelmsleben* (*Guillaume d'Angleterre*). These are the "large"
editions. All except the *Lancelot* were later reissued in "small
editions" for use in classes, without critical apparatus, and sometimes without glossaries: the *Erec and Enide* in 1896, 1909,
and 1934; the *Cligés in* 1888, 1901, 1910, 1921, and abridged
editions by A. HILKA and H. BREUER in 1934; *Yvain* in 1891,
1902, 1906, 1912, and without glossary in 1913—revision by
A. HILKA in 1926; *Guillaume d'Angleterre,* 1911.
Les romans de Chretien de Troyes. ("Classiques français du moyen-
âge" series.) Paris: Champion, 1952–64. Vol. I (1952), *Erec
et Enide,* ed. MARIO ROQUES; Vol. II (1958), *Cligés,* ed. ALEX-
ANDER MICHA; Vol. III (1962), *Chevalier de la Charette,* ed.
MARIO ROQUES; Vol. IV (1964, 1965, 1967), *Le Chevalier au
Lion (Yvain),* ed. MARIO ROQUES.
Guillaume d'Angleterre, ed. MAURICE WILMOTTE. ("Classiques fran-
çais du moyen-âge" series.) Paris: Champion, 1927.
Philomena, ed. CORNELIUS DEBOER. Paris: Geuthner, 1909. A good
text.
Le roman de Perceval, ed. WILLIAM ROACH. Geneva; Paris: Librairie
Droz; Librairie Minard, 1959. The best edition.
Der Percevalroman (*Li Contes del Graal*) *von Christian von Troyes,*

ed. ALFONS HILKA. Halle: Niemeyer, 1932. Edition made to complete series begun by Wendelin Foerster in 1884.

4. Editions of Other Romances Associated with Problems in Chrétien Studies

The Continuators of the Old French Perceval of Chrétien de Troyes, ed. WILLIAM J. ROACH. 3 vols.; Philadelphia: University of Pennsylvania Press, 1949–. First volume contains First Continuation as found in MSS A, L, P, R, S, with a glossary prepared by LUCIEN FOULET; second volume represents the same continuation as found in MSS E, M, Q, U; third volume in process of preparation.

GERBERT DE MONTREUIL, La continuation de Perceval, ed. MARY WILLIAMS. ("Classiques français du moyen âge" series.) 2 vols.; Paris: Champion, 1922–25. Only 14,078 verses included; third volume not yet published.

ROBERT DE BORON, Le roman de l'Estoire dou Graal, ed. W. A. NITZE. ("Classiques français du moyen âge" series.) Paris: Champion, 1927. Standard edition; contains also what remains of the Merlin.

The Didot Perceval, ed. WILLIAM ROACH. Philadelphia: University of Pennsylvania Press, 1941. Fine edition.

Le Haut Livre du Graal: Perlesvaus, ed. WILLIAM A. NITZE and others, 2 vols.; Chicago: 1932–37. Numerous collaborators, including T. A. JENKINS, W. VON WARTBURG, and WILLIAM ROACH.

The Vulgate Version of the Arthurian Romances, edited from manuscripts in the British Museum, by H. OSKAR SOMMER. 7 vols.; Washington: Carnegie Institute, 1909–13. Only edition of the complete Vulgate Prose Romances; tremendous work.

5. General Studies on Chrétien de Troyes

COHEN, GUSTAVE. Un grand romancier d'amour et d'aventure au douzième siècle. Paris: Boivin, 1931. A general appreciation of the poet, with many analyses at length.

FOERSTER, WENDELIN, Kristian von Troyes, Wörterbuch. Halle: Niemeyer, 1914. Gives survey of Foerster's opinions; contains also a most useful glossary of the vocabulary which Chrétien used, and an Index of Proper Names.

FRAPPIER, JEAN. Chrétien de Troyes, l'homme et l'œuvre. Paris:

Selected Bibliography

Hatier-Boivin, 1957. More of a compilation than this present work of ours; presents somewhat different overall point of view.

HOFER, STEFAN. *Christian de Troyes: Leben und Werke des altfranzösischen Epikers.* Graz-Köln: Hermann Böhlau Nachf., 1954. A much appreciated study.

HOLMES, URBAN T., and SISTER AMELIA KLENKE, O. P. *Chrétien, Troyes, and the Grail.* Chapel Hill: University of North Carolina Press, 1959. Although much of this concerns the Grail, there are fresh ideas on Chrétien de Troyes in general, and on his surroundings.

6. Chrétien's Perceval, or Conte dou Graal

FRAPPIER, JEAN. *Le Roman breton: Chrétien de Troyes, Perceval ou le Conte du Graal.* Paris: Centre de Documentation Universitaire, 1953. Very useful work; minimizes symbolism and places more emphasis on psychology of the age.

KAHANE, HENRY R., AND RENÉE. *The Krater and the Grail, Hermetic Studies of the Parzival.* Urbana: University of Illinois Press, 1965. Although Wolfram's *Parzival* is main subject, Chrétien's *Perceval* is included.

KLENKE, SISTER M. AMELIA, O. P. *Liturgy and Allegory in Chretien's Perceval.* Chapel Hill: UNC Studies in the Romance Languages and Literatures, 1951. Should be read in conjunction with Holmes and Klenke, *Chrétien, Troyes, and the Grail* (see above).

OLSCHKI, LEONARDO. *The Grail Castle and its Mysteries, with Preface by Eugene Vinaver,* trans. J. A. SCOTT. Manchester: Manchester University Press, 1966. Argues idea of Gnostic sources for Grail; includes new material.

WESTON, JESSIE L. *From Ritual to Romance.* Cambridge: the University Press, 1920. Most significant presentation of Ritualist theory for origins of Grail.

7. Miscellaneous Studies

FLUTRE, LOUIS FERNAND. *Table des noms propres . . . dans les romans du moyen âge.* Poitiers: Centre d'Etudes supérieures de civilisation médiévale, 1962. Invaluable reference work; speaks for itself.

FOURRIER, ANTHIME. "Encore la chronologie des œuvres de Chrétien de Troyes"; *Bulletin bibliographique de la Societe internationale Arthurienne*, II (1950, 69–88). Supplemented by JEAN MISRAHI, *ibid.*, XI (1959), 89–120. Gives the more or less prevailing view of the chronology of Chrétien's works; differs somewhat from dating preferred by the present author.

GUYER, FOSTER E. "The Influence of Ovid on Chrétien de Troyes," *Romanic Review*, XII (1921) 97–247. Abstract of University of Chicago dissertation; more or less the classic study on Chrétien and Ovid; was reprinted for private distribution.

KÖHLER, ERICH. *Ideal und Wirklichkeit in der höfischen Epik.* Tübingen: Heft 97 of the *Beihefte, Ztschr, fur rom. Philologie*, 1966. Very sensitive critique.

PARIS, GASTON. *Mélanges de littérature française du moyen âge.* Paris: Champion, 1910. Reprint of articles by the great master; few of them have to do with his views on Chrétien de Troyes.

La Concordance de Philomena de Chrétien de Troyes. L' Université de Liège, 1969. All of Chrétien's romances will be so treated.

Index

Abduction of Guenevere, 24, 97
Abrams, Phyllis, 33
Adelard of Bath, 30
Adèle of Champagne: Queen of France, 31
Adolf, Helen, 141
Adonis cult, 142, 143
Adoration of the Cross, 147
Agnes: Sister of Philip Augustus, 30
Alberic de Bezinzô, 36–7, 147 n. 11
Albigensians, 147, 168
Alexander, 36–7, 59
Alix: Daughter of Louis VII, 31
Allegory, 141, 154, 165, 158
Androcles and the Lion, 111
Aneirin, 38
Anglo-Normans, 29, 32
Apuleius, 85, 148
Aristotle, 35–6, 169
Ars amatoria: summary of, 48–8
Arthurian legend considered false *See* preface, 39, 112–3
Arthur's grave, 39
Arthur: historicity of, 38–9
Arthurian literature: beginning of, 38–9
Artorius, 38
Athis et Prophilias, 19
Attic Nights, 111
Auerbach, Erich, 115, 173 n. 1
Aulus Gellius, 111
Avalon, 69

Badon Hill, 38
Baile in Scáil, 145
Bar-le-Duc, 84
Bar-sur-Aube, 23
Baudri de Bourgueil, 33
Bayrav, Süheyla, 113–4
Beaus Desconeus, 96
Beauty description, 53
Beauvais, 14; cathedral, 78, 80
Benecke, G. F., 104
Benton, John, 23, 172 n. 18
Bernart de Ventadorn, 57

Béroul, 79
Blanchefleur: chastity of, 158
Bleeding Lance: most significant, 157, 161
Bogdanow, Fanni, 137
Bran, 144
Breri (Bledhericus), 52
Bretagne: matière de, 28
Breton conteurs, 145
Brittany, 27, 31
Broceliande, meaning of, 112–3
Bron, *see* Fisher King
Brown, A. C. L., 116, 117
Bruce, James Douglas, Preface, 184
Brut, 39, 41, 50, 59, 110; Welsh *Bruts*, 179 n. 4
Burdach, Konrad, 139
Bury–St. Edmund's, 119
Byzantine, 27, 37, 73, 84–5, 125–6, 168; legends, 24–5; Mass, 142
Byzantium, 27, 28–9, 30

Caballero de Cifar, 125
Calendre, 40
Camelot, 89
Canterbury "group," 30
Caradoc, 24, 69, 99
Carinthia, 84–5
Carlisle, 30
Carmody, Francis, 182 n. 24
Cart, in *Lancelot*, 98–99
Celtic, themes, 18, 21, 60–1, 67–8, 101, 140, 144, 155; peoples, 27, 168
Celtic explanations of Grail, 144–6
Celtisants, 144–5, 146
Chambers, E. K., 184
Champagne, 27
Chansonniers, 16
Characters, from many sources, 96
Charity, 139, 161, 162–4, 169
Chaumont, 22
Chevalier au Cygne, 67
Chivalry, 29

Index

Foerster, Wendelin, 12, 19, 50, 53, 77, 118, 185
Folk motifs, 96 ff., 99–100, 11, 168
"Food producer," 143
Foster, I. L., 151
Fourrier, Anthime, 21, 59, 187-8
Franciscans, 34
Frappier, Jean, Preface, 20–1, 115, 120, 140–1, 186–7
Frederick Barbarossa, 29, 31
Free Will, 147–8
Futerer, Ulrich, 88

Galloway, 126, 155
Games, 53
Ganymede, 149
Gawain, 83
Gawain episodes, 140–1
General agreement of scholars, 21
Genisa, *see* Fénice, 85
Genuflection, 93, 101, 147
Geoffrey of Monmouth, 24, 67
Geraint: name, 71
Gerald the Welshman, Preface, 52, 112, 182 n. 11
Gérard of Liège, 36
Gerbert (de Montreuil), 14, 133, 135, 186
Germany, 27
Gerould, Gordon Hall, 125
Giants, 182 n. 9; in *Erec and Enide*, 64, 71
Gildas, 38
Girart de Roussillon, 140
Glastonbury 24, 51, 60, 67, 70, 126, 142, 146, 153
Gnostics, 147, 150, 168
God as Light, 147
Godefroy de Leigny, 15, 188
Godefroy of Bouillon, 28
Gododdin, 38
Golden Legend, 164
Goosens, Heinrich, 117
Gorre, 89, 90, 92, 93, 99, 100–101
Gottfried von Strassburg, 79
goy (Jewish term of opprobrium, often applied to one who had deserted the faith), 53
Grace, 61, 113, 114, 155, 158, 159
Grail bearer, 140, 145, 149

Grail Castle, or Hall, 142, 145, 158, 160, 163, 167; allegory, 158
Grail Procession, 141, 142, 163–4
Grail Vessel 153; embellishment, 166; etymology, 165–6; description, 140, 156; symbol, 140
Grail and Crusaders, 141, 182 n. 24
Gröber, Gustav, 119
Gronw, 143
Guenevere, 44, 71; her comb, 44, 90
Guillaume d'Angleterre, 18, 16, 17, 20–1, 40; summary, 121–4; MS C, 120; Spanish prose version, 120–1; Scottish names, 126, 180 n. 7
Guillaume de Saint-Thierry, 35–6
"guilt feeling," 61
Guyer, Foster E., 79, 175 n. 1, 188

Hadrian, Pope, 29
Hamilton, G. L., 116–7
Harris, Julian, 25, 113
Hartmann von Aue, 71, 104, 117
Hatzfeld, Helmut, 182 n. 24
Hebrews, Epistle to the, 167
Helie de Borron (Missire), 137
Helinandus of Froidmont (Aisne), 140, 154, 166
Henry of Blois, Bishop, 24, 60
Henry I of Champagne, 23, 31–2, 84, 161; marriage, 18, 19, 20
Henry II of England, 30, 60, 139, 154
Herald, Chrétien as a, 17, 20
Herman of Laon, 39
Hideous Damsel, 145, 155, 158, 161
Hoepffner, Ernest, 170 n. 6
Hofer, Stefan, 20, 59, 68, 84, 139, 187
Holmes, U. T., 171–2 n. 16, 187
Holy Land, 18
Hortus deliciarum, M.S., 141
Horus, 150
Hospitable host motif, 71
Hungary, 28
Huon de Méry, 114
Huth Merlin, 136–7
Hyginus, 49–50

Ireland, 27, 145

Index

Merlin, 159
Metamorphoses, 148–9
Metamorphosis, see Apuleius
Meun-sur-Loire, 33
Meyer, Paul, 120, 135
Micha, Alexandre, 170
Micyllus, 50
Misrahi, Jean, 171 n. 13, n. 15, 188
Mockery of Arthur, 112–3
Modena sculptures, 87, 174 n. 11
Morgant la Fée, 68, 71
Mort Artu, 69, 136
Motif Index, 50

Neckam, Alexander, 114
Nelli, René, 146–7
Nennius, 38
Neoplatonism, 36, 148
Newstead, Helaine, 182 n. 5
New Testament, 160, 164
Nichols, Stephen G., 175 n. 10
Nitze, W. A., 97, 116, 142–3, 159, 160, 186, 177 n. 17, n. 18
Nûr-ed-Din, 18, 19, 104

Old Rome vs. Modern, 46–47
Old Testament, 148, 160
Olschki, Leonardo, 147–8, 150, 187
Orgueilleus: as a name, 155, 175
Oriental tales, 18, 146, 150
Orthodox Christian instruction, 148
Osiris, 143, 150
Ovid, 14, 17, 18, 33–4, 48; quite modern, 17, 48
Ovide moralisé, 53
Owls, 53
"Oyster," 156

Parallel, 26; between Gawain and Perceval, 158
Paris, Gaston, 17–18, 50, 53, 77, 188
Parry, John J., 178 n. 3, 185
Paton, Lucy A., 116
Pauphilet, Albert, 98–9, 179 n. 4
Pelops, 15, 17; summary, 49–50
Perceval, 68, 83, 145; name meaning, 69, 156, 158

Perceval or *Conte dou Graal*, 14, 16, 18, 35, 68, 126, 135, 143, 147, 155, 157–60, 164; summary, 127–33; Christian interpretation, 137–41
Peredur, 150–1
Perilous Ford, 126, 132, 155
Perlesvaus, 136, 159, 160, 186
Persia, 146–7
Peter Comestor, 22
Phallic rite, 142, 150
Philip Augustus: instruction book, 153
Philip of Flanders: book of, 18, 20, 21, 25, 139, 151, 160–1
Philomena, 18, 20, 40, 52–4, 188
Placides–Eustachius legend, 121, 124; summary, 124–125
Plato, 169
Plato: the devil, 54
Platter, 144, 166
Plerome, 148
Ponsoye, Pierre, 146
Pope, Arthur U., 146–7
Prose Tristan, 136–7
Pryderi–Perceval, 144
Pseudo–Robert of Boron Cycle, 136–7
Pseudo–Walter Mapes Cycle, 136–7
Pseudo–Wauchier, 135
Psychology: medieval, 169
Purple-fringed garments, 136
Pyramus et Thisbé, 34

Quest, "purifying," 60–1
Queste del Saint Graal, 159

Raimbaut d'Aurenga, 58
Rauch, 117
Raynaud, Gaston, 55
Reason, J. H., 113
Remedy of Love, of Ovid, 42; summary, 43–4
Rhymed chronicles: form of, 34, 36–7
Richard: King of England, 31
Richard de Fournival, 50
Richard of Saint-Victor, 35
Rion or Rithon, 155, 162
Ritualist Theory, of Grail, 141

Index

DATE DUE